UNDER THE WIRES AT TALLY HO

TRAMWAYS

METROPOLITAN ELECTRIC · LONDON UNITED · SOUTH METROPOLITAN ELECTRIC

TROLLEYBUS

UNDER THE WIRES AT TALLY HO

TRAMS AND TROLLEYBUSES OF NORTH LONDON 1905–1962

DAVID BERGUER

The
History
Press

First published 2010

The History Press
The Mill, Brimscombe Port
Stroud, Gloucestershire, GL5 2QG
www.thehistorypress.co.uk

British Library Cataloguing in Publication Data.
A catalogue record for this book is available from the British Library.

ISBN 978 0 7524 5875 5

Typesetting and origination by The History Press
Printed in Great Britain
Manufacturing managed by Jellyfish Print Solutions Ltd

CONTENTS

REFLECTIONS

A tribute to the London trolleybus (not forgetting the dear old trams):

A distant singing in the wires
And the sound of rubber tyres,
She hoves in view, no mess or fuss
The London Transport trolleybus.
Slowing now from those who race;
Gliding in with style and pace.
Thankful for a pleasant ride.
In standard red she looks so grand,
With down her length a neat cream band.
Step aboard and take a seat
With safety rails and patterns neat.
Seating for three score and ten
To terminus and back again.
Climb the stairway; look around
A better view high off the ground.
No need for lines to guide the way
The trackless vehicle now holds sway,
No hill or vale will worry her.
With powerful motor's steady purr
She travels on with high esteem
To take her place in the transport scene.
The trams before had served us well
With clanking wheels and clanging bell.
As 'electrics' came upon the scene
To places where we had not been
They opened up a wider scheme
And some fulfilled a waiting dream.
As time moved on and lines went far.
For those of us without a car
Could travel to our work each day
And have more time in which to play.
As public transport played its part
The engineers and those in art
And so good friend you carved your name;
Brought in an age when in its prime
Pullman trams now on the line
Years ahead beyond their time.
With population growing fast
We asked how long that this could last
With competition gaining hold
A new-found plan would now unfold;

And so in nineteen thirty three
We saw the name LPTB.
New ideas with some in haste
The tramcar soon would be replaced.
A new type vehicle we will see
With charm and grace and dignity,
A six wheeled giant now would be shown
With speed and power as yet unknown.
While some change gear and others try
The trolleybus goes sailing by.
Growing now from strength to strength
With names emblazoned down her length,
New routes planned are now unfurled
The largest system in the world.
Through war-time London safely brought
They carried on when fuel was short.
At football matches we would see
They moved the crowds efficiently.
Used by many, not just the few
We journeyed off to pastures new,
From leafy lanes to the city's swell,
This silent workhorse served us well.
But later on, beyond our fears,
We entered the affluent years.
More private transport would appear,
The future too becoming clear,
While winding down was taking place
Others too would join the race.
The trolleybus has passed its prime
Just a question now of time.
And so in nineteen sixty two
We said goodbye to one so true
The system closed and final days
Saw great events in different ways.
And so good friend you carved your name;
The London scene won't be the same
You played your part through sun and rain.
Will we see your like again?
In this modern age we need
To stop and think as once decreed.
As I look back on happier time,
I think it best to end this rhyme.
I found contentment in my abode
When the trolleybus once ruled the road.

© Ron Kingdon

INTRODUCTION

I have been interested in transport for as long as I can remember, but my involvement in local history only began in 1990, when I took early retirement and was searching for something that was not too demanding to occupy me. I joined the Friern Barnet & District Local History Society or, rather, I helped to form it, since it then consisted of a handful of people who were only just thinking about setting up a group to look into the history of the area.

Our area of interest covers the boundaries of the old Friern Barnet & District Urban District Council which was swept away in the changes to local government in 1965 and became part of the London Borough of Barnet. The 'and District' part in the Society's name covers New Southgate, North Finchley and Whetstone so this book covers the operation of trams and trolleybuses in this area, but it ranges as far north as Barnet and as far south as Central London.

There have been many admirable books on London's transport and many of them tend to concentrate on the vehicles themselves. It would be pointless to go over ground already covered by Ken Blacker in his excellent books *The London Trolleybus Volumes 1 and 2* and C.S. Smeeton's exhaustive *The Metropolitan Electric Tramways Volumes 1 and 2*, so I have tried to paint a different picture, one that would chronicle the events surrounding the introduction and subsequent operation of trams and trolleybuses, and also try and capture the feel of the times. For those of you who are more technically minded, I have included brief details of the vehicles and routes in the appendices. I have also included details of bus routes so that the kind of competition the trams faced can be more easily seen. Thanks are due to the tireless work of the London Historical Research Group of the Omnibus Society for this information and to David Ruddom for kindly supplying it. I also have devoted one chapter to the workings of the pirate bus operators as their short-lived activities initially affected tram operators in London.

I am indebted to several people whose knowledge is much greater than mine and whose help has therefore been invaluable: Ron Kingdon for his reminiscences and photographs; Hugh Taylor who knows more about trolleybuses than practically anyone else; Alan Williams whose love of trams, particular those of MET, was an inspiration; Fred Ivey for his infallible memories of his days spent photographing London's buses and trams; Percy Reboul for allowing me to use his oral histories of tram drivers; Richard Testar for his reminiscences of boyhood days riding on trolleybuses; Beatrice Dobie for her memories of her grandfather; and for everyone who has allowed me to use their memories. Special thanks go to Yasmine Webb and Hugh Petrie of Barnet Local Studies and Archives, who patiently put up with me spending hours in their company. My thanks are also due to Mel Hooper and the late John Donovan of the Friern Barnet & District Local History Society for their support and encouragement.

No transport history would be complete without photographs of the vehicles themselves and my thanks are due to all the photographers who spent many hours on the streets of London recording trams and trolleybuses and incidentally capturing the surrounding street scenes. I have acknowledged the source of the photographs and am particularly grateful to Transport for London for permission to use their copyright photographs which are lodged in the London Transport Museum collection.

Special thanks are due to my wife Patricia who not only put up with being dragged round various transport museums and being forced to ride on ancient vehicles without complaining, but also acted as my proofreader.

I hope that not too many errors have crept into the text; if you spot any please contact me at davidberguer@hotmail.com and I will include any revisions in future editions of this work.

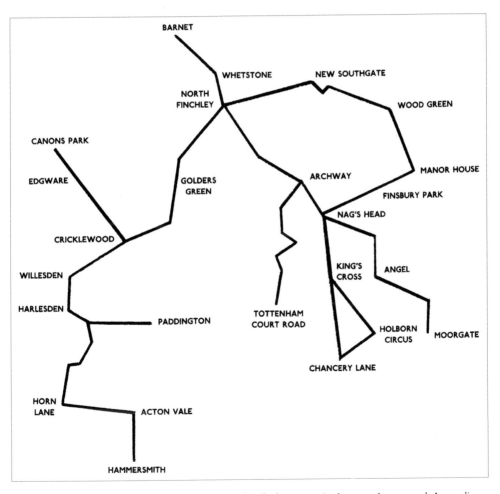

Tram and trolleybus routes. For full details of tram and trolleybus routes in the area, please consult Appendices 2 and 5 on pages 107 and 120.

CHAPTER 1

A PROTRACTED BIRTH

The *Barnet Press* of 3 June 1905 carried the following editorial comment:

> For our part we are firmly convinced that the tramcars will actually be in full swing some day.
> In any case we ought to be grateful to whoever has this enterprise in hand for adding to our
> limited stock of figures of speech. Nowadays when Finchley people want to indicate a date
> that will never arrive they say 'when the tramcars are running'.

The timing of this remark was somewhat odd because exactly a week later, under the heading
'Electric Cars at Last', the paper reported that 'the ratepayers of Finchley and that part of
Hornsey which borders on the Archway-road had the pleasure of the cars started for service on
Wednesday at midday.'

So what had led to this sense of frustration? Why did it take so long for trams to come
to Finchley? After all, the London Street Tramways and the North Metropolitan had been
running trams from Central London to the Archway Tavern since 1874. Admittedly these
were horse-drawn, but they were still quicker and more comfortable than the horse-drawn
omnibuses that the people of Finchley and district were forced to use.

It was around the end of the nineteenth century that electric tramways became a real possibility
and the newly formed London County Council (LCC) introduced its first electric tram in 1901.
However, as early as 1899, Finchley Urban District Council was resisting proposals by Middlesex
County Council (MCC) for the construction of an electric tramway. This was because Finchley
Council wanted to build its own tramway. The Finchley Council minutes of 12 April 1899 record:

> The committee recommended that it be referred to the Clerk and Surveyor to take such steps as
> they may consider necessary for promoting a scheme of Light Railways under the Light Railways
> Act between the Boundary of the District with Hornsey at the Archway Road to Totteridge
> Lane and that application for an order enabling the Council to construct a Light Railway to be
> made to the Light Railway Commissioners in May next and that in his discretion the Clerk to
> be authorised to instruct Mr Forbes to act on behalf of the Council in carrying out this proposal.

On 29 May 1899 Finchley resolved:

> That in reply to the letter from the Middlesex County Council dated 4th inst a letter be sent
> that this Council are themselves applying in conjunction with the Hornsey Urban District

Council for an order authorising the construction of light railways through the district between the Archway Tavern and the Boundary of the District with Barnet that the Council have determined upon any scheme this Council would be glad to confer with them generally.

It is worth recalling that Middlesex then covered virtually a quarter of outer North London from the River Colne in the west to the River Lea in the east and from the River Thames in the south to Potters Bar in the north. The MCC was therefore a very powerful body and, as well as controlling services like education and public health, was also responsible for the upkeep of roads and bridges. Not surprisingly, in this battle of David and Goliath, the big guy would win and the dispute between Finchley Council and Middlesex was only going to end one way.

In 1899, the MCC applied to the Railway Commissioners for an order authorising the construction of a light railway ('light railways' included tramways). Although the MCC would build the lines and make the necessary infrastructure improvements, they would not operate the tramways themselves, but would grant a lease to Metropolitan Electric Tramways (MET), part of the British Electric Traction (BET) Group, which would expire at the end of 1930. MET would supply and operate the generating equipment and overhead wires and supply and operate the tramcars themselves and maintain the track.

The turn of the century was the time when electricity was just starting to find its way into all aspects of life, not just transport, and private firms and local councils were all anxious to promote its use. Whilst Finchley Council's desire to operate its own electric tramway might be put down to a sense of self-importance, they actually saw it as an excellent opportunity to use some of the power from their own generating station in Squires Lane. At this time, of course, few homes had electricity and those that did only used it for lighting as domestic appliances had not yet arrived, so the demand for power was heavily biased towards the hours of darkness; clearly a tramway operating throughout the day would prove to be an excellent way of smoothing out demand. However, in a report to Finchley Council dated 12 March 1907, their chief electrical engineer stated that they had 1,111 customers (out of a population of around 12,000) together with 661 public lamps and a total of 40,652 lamps of 8-candlepower and, with an estimated 20,000 lamps needing to be supplied by the end of 1909, the existing generating capacity was insufficient and that new plant would have to be installed at a cost of £18,808 (equivalent to around £880,000 today). Thus can be seen the futility of local councils trying to supply their own electricity.

Finchley briefly had the support of Hornsey Council for the construction of a tram line from Archway northwards to Finchley and Whetstone, but when this support was withdrawn, they finally capitulated, but not without some continued sniping. The council minute for 5 March 1900 states:

On the motion of Mr Todd seconded Mr Paul. Urgency be declared for a motion that the Council is of the opinion that the Cross Country scheme of Light Railways as promoted by the Middlesex County Council and the Tramways & Omnibus Co. Limited in their order No.1 and by the Middlesex County Council in their order No. 2 is at present unnecessary and unlikely to be remunerative so far as such schemes affect the District of Finchley this Council is of the opinion:

1.   That the proposed Railway in Oakleigh Road is unnecessary.

2.   That the proposed Railway in Woodhouse Lane is unnecessary.

3.   The proposed Railway along Ballards Lane and Regents Park Road, without means of access to London, is useless and the expense of its construction will be wholly out of comparison with a revenue dividend from purely local traffic.

On 20 May 1905 the *Finchley Press* commented:

One fact that ought not to be forgotten, in connection with Finchley's electric trams, is that it is largely – indeed we may say entirely – due to the vigorous action of Mr Todd and those councillors who supported his policy that the current is to be supplied by the Finchley Council's electricity department. One of the reasons why the Council fought so tenaciously for the control of the trams in Finchley was that by supplying the power for the trams the Council would be able to generate the total current consumed in the parish at a cheaper rate than they otherwise would, and thus the individual consumer and the ratepayers as a whole would be the gainers. Although the Council did not succeed in its efforts to become the tramway authority in Finchley, it is some satisfaction that the electrical power used in driving the cars is to be purchased from the Council.

Before the coming of the trams, the horse bus was the only form of mass public road transport. As can be seen here, the state of the road surface at the edges forced what little traffic there was to keep to the centre. (Commercial postcard)

A track-laying gang pauses for a photograph in North Finchley in 1904. (John Heathfield Collection)

However, the victory was to be relatively short-lived. In 1904 Northmet, a sister company of MET, had opened its own power station at Brimsdown which supplied the required power not only to other MET lines in Wood Green and Edmonton but also to domestic consumers in a large area of West Essex, South Hertfordshire and North Middlesex. The Finchley lines were eventually supplied by Northmet from Brimsdown from about 1908 onwards. In fact, the tramways were to consume 50 per cent of Northmet's generating capacity until 1914.

Another cause of delay was the siting of a depot for the trams. When the MET were first considering building a tramway in the area they looked at several sites. Church End and East End Road were considered, but in 1903 they finally decided in favour of a site at Tally Ho Corner. Protracted negotiations with the site's owner, the local builder C.F. Day, meant that work did not begin until September 1904. The depot backed onto Christchurch Avenue and a new road, Rosemont Avenue, had been specially constructed to facilitate access via Woodberry Grove. The new depot, which opened on 7 June 1905, had been built at a cost of over £18,000, had room for sixty cars and there were fifteen tracks inside.

CHAPTER 2

THE TRAMS AT LAST

On Wednesday 7 June 1905 car No.125 was inspected at Finchley depot and then made a trial run to the terminus at a point opposite The Green Man in Whetstone and then down the Great North Road to Archway, after which it entered public service at noon. The trams terminated under Archway Bridge, which was the boundary between Middlesex and the LCC area. Passengers wishing to continue their journey into London were obliged to walk down to the bottom of Archway Road where they could then catch an LCC horse-drawn tram. In the same week the *Finchley Press* reported:

> A correspondent calls our attention to the notice affixed to the centre poles and containing the information where trams will stop for passengers to alight. The writer says he took a friend the other night after dark to show him the various stopping places along the High Road. To his amazement he found these important notice boards were useless after daylight. The electric lights are so attached to the centre poles that the necessary information to persons willing to know where they can enter the trams or alight is obscured. This is comforting information for dark winter nights.

Despite this small criticism, business was brisk and there were long queues throughout the day until the trams ceased shortly after 11p.m. Not surprisingly, the horse-drawn omnibuses soon reduced their fares in competition but the local paper reported that few people patronised them. Trams ran every few minutes, and the fares, which were a penny cheaper than the horse buses had been charging, were:

Whetstone to Squires Lane	1*d*
Tally Ho Corner to East Finchley	1*d*
Squires Lane to Muswell Hill Road	1*d*
East Finchley Station to Archway	1*d*
Whetstone to Highgate Station	2*d*
Tally Ho Corner to Archway	2*d*
All the way	3*d*

Workmen's cars from Whetstone ran from 5a.m. till 7.27a.m. The first car from Highgate left at 5.35a.m. The last car 'down' was at 11.47 and the last car 'up' was at 11.12p.m. Journey time from Whetstone to Highgate was 30 minutes.

The first tram, No.125, poses for the camera with MET men outnumbering local urchins by two to one. (Andrew Forsyth Collection)

Initially the service was operated by twenty-seven tramcars costing £800 each. Each tram could carry sixty-eight passengers, thirty inside and thirty-eight on the upper deck. Although passengers riding upstairs did so without any form of cover and on wooden slatted seats, those choosing to sit inside could do so on upholstered benches which ran the length of the car; they even had heavy curtains at the windows and cut glass lampshades. Trams were noisy, but they were quick, frequent, brightly lit and cheap. Within a week, horse buses were being described as 'dull and antiquated and cumbrous and generally antediluvian. The very horses seem to have an extra air of despondency as they toilsomely climb the hill up from East Finchley Station.'

On Whit Monday, the cars were crowded all day and people wishing to ride had to wait in some instances nearly an hour. At one time no less than 700 people were waiting at the Whetstone terminus and there were big crowds at Tally Ho Corner and at the Bald Faced Stag in East Finchley.

Within a few weeks, horse bus fares were reduced again to half their original level, but they had already lost the battle for passengers. The whole aspect of the highway had been transformed. The thoroughfare was crowded, the whole locality was animated, and people were taking rides – especially women with babies – just for the fun of the thing. The most up-to-date saying at the time in Finchley was, 'Have you had a ride on the tram?'

On 24 June the *Finchley Press* reported that all buses plying between Charing Cross and North Finchley were being withdrawn and put on the route to Muswell Hill with the probability that a service of buses would be started along Colney Hatch Lane. Not surprisingly, some enterprising local businessmen were soon taking advantage of the new tram service. On 8 July an advertisement for property in Squires Lane appeared saying, 'Cheapest Villas in North London. Just off electric tram route.'

THE METROPOLITAN ELECTRIC TRAMWAYS, LTD.

Whetstone and
Highgate.

THE OPENING OF THIS LINE WILL TAKE PLACE ON

WEDNESDAY, 7th JUNE, 1905.

ELECTRIC CARS

Will be run every few minutes from WHETSTONE about 12.30 noon up to 11.0 p.m.
Last Car from HIGHGATE 11.35 p.m.

ON AND AFTER

THURSDAY, 8th JUNE, 1905,

The Service will be run at frequent intervals, as under:

Leave WHETSTONE.	Leave HIGHGATE ARCHWAY.
First Car ... ... 5. 0 a.m.	First Car ... ... 5.35 a.m.
Last Car ... ... 11.12 p.m.	Last Car ... ... 11.47 p.m.

FARES either way between,

Whetstone and Squires Lane	**1**d.
Tally Ho Corner and East Finchley Station	**1**d.
Squires Lane and Muswell Hill Road	**1**d.
East Finchley Station and Highgate	**1**d.
Whetstone and Muswell Hill Road...	**2**d.
Tally Ho Corner and Highgate	**2**d.
Whetstone and Highgate	**3**d.

WORKMEN'S CARS

Will leave WHETSTONE at 5.0, 5.35, 6.10, 6.45, 7.0, 7.9, 7.18, 7.27 a.m.
Will leave HIGHGATE at 5.35, 6.10, 6.45, 7.20 a.m.

FARES by Workmen's Cars:

SINGLE JOURNEY (any distance) **1**d.   **TWO JOURNEY TICKET 2**d.

N.B.—TWO JOURNEY TICKETS issued on this Line are available for a second journey either way
on any of the Company's Cars running between HIGHGATE and WHETSTONE at any time
(Sundays. Good Friday, Christmas Day, and Bank Holidays excepted).

Cars will stop to take up or let down **Passengers** at the specified **Stopping Places only.**

Passengers will please notify the Conductor of their intention to alight **before** reaching such **Stopping Places,** and are cautioned against attempting to enter or leave the Cars when in motion.

TRAFFIC OFFICES (TEMPORARY)—   *By Order,* W. E. HAMMOND,
  52-54, LORDSHIP LANE, WOOD GREEN, N.   Traffic Manager.
3rd June, 1905.

Daniel Greenaway & Sons, Printers, London, E.C.

B306 20M 6 05

The top deck may have been cold and uncomfortable, but the interior was sumptuous, with padded seats. (London Borough of Barnet Archives)

The first serious accident involving a tram took place on the second morning of operation at North Finchley, outside the offices of the *Finchley Press*, which must have pleased the reporters. A horse bus was heading towards Charing Cross, followed by a tram. The tram driver rang his bell but there was a collision and the tram forced the bus on to the pathway, ripping the stairs completely off in the process. The ironwork of the steps at the front of the tram was slightly damaged and had to be forced off with a piece of iron. Fortunately, the bus conductor was inside the vehicle and escaped unhurt. The only passenger, a lady from Friern Park, was said to be 'so severely shaken that she had to be removed to her house in a cab'. There is no record of what happened to the horse; hopefully it survived uninjured. In July a less fortunate beast had both knees chipped and the inside of its hocks cut when the hay cart it was pulling was hit by tramcar No.130 near Woodside Lane. The front of the tram was damaged but the cart completely overturned and the nearside axle was broken.

Accidents like this were almost inevitable; until the coming of the trams nearly all vehicles were horse-drawn and even those were few and far between. Photographs from the period show pedestrians strolling unconcernedly in the middle of the road and they were easily able to avoid what little traffic there was. Small boys, as mischievous as ever, soon discovered a new pastime. An East Finchley correspondent, writing in June, said: 'I saw three boys under the railway bridge, and one of them lodged a stone in the tram line with the evident intention of trying to send the tram off the line.' The correspondent suggested that other boys may attempt the same dangerous practice, and they should be warned of the serious consequences.

Just before the MET's Archway – Whetstone line opened, the LCC had commissioned the building of a short stretch of track to link the MET line at the Archway Bridge to the end of their line at Archway Tavern at the foot of the hill. This line would have overhead wires, allowing MET trams to continue through to the LCC's tracks. The line opened to the public on Friday 22 December 1905 and, despite the extra journey, fares remained the same and traffic boomed, so much so that an extra six cars were allocated to the route, bringing the number up to thirty-three.

The aftermath of the crash at Archway. (Commercial postcard)

This early view of Archway looking north shows how the tram would have come straight down Archway Road to meet its fate. Nowadays the Archway Tavern stands in the middle of a large traffic island. (Andrew Forsyth Collection)

This short stretch of track was particularly steep (one in twenty-two) and at first it was considered that the existing brakes, which operated only on the wheels of the vehicles, would be adequate, but magnetic brakes, which clamped down onto the track itself, were soon fitted. Despite this, a serious accident occurred at 3.35p.m. on Saturday 23 June 1906 when car No.115 was descending the hill. Just south of the bridge it collided with a hearse, and on the corner of Harburton Road it struck an empty furniture van, wrecking them both. The motorman jumped off the tram and it picked up speed and, near the bottom of the hill it hit a Vanguard motor bus which was carried across the pavement and into a restaurant, killing three pedestrians in the process. Fortunately the bus was only carrying five people, four of them on the lower deck. Car No.115 then struck another tramcar which was stationary at the terminus and, such was the speed of the runaway tram that the two of them continued on for another 120ft into Holloway Road, where they came to rest against the kerb, demolishing a lamp standard and a post in the process.

At the subsequent Board of Trade enquiry, the motorman, thirty-year-old Ernest Cone, said he had noticed that the wheels had locked when he had braked near Shepherds Hill but the car had eventually stopped at the Winchester Hotel. He reported that the rails were greasy and when he subsequently tried to brake at Archway Bridge the wheels locked again. He put the controller into reverse and the circuit breaker blew, so the magnetic brake could not be applied. At this point he saw the furniture van ahead and decided to vacate his position. There had been twenty-five passengers on board, plus the conductor, Griffith Davies, who was praised for persuading most of them to stay on board. Nevertheless, four or five of them jumped off when the car began its descent and were injured, although not fatally. The report recommended that, in future, the magnetic track brakes should be used as a matter of course, not just in emergencies. This was later adopted as standard practice by the MET and subsequently rheostatic braking was introduced, which operated on the motors themselves.

CHAPTER 3
THE SYSTEM EXPANDS

At the northern end of the line, work had started on an extension from The Green Man at Whetstone northwards to the county boundary with Hertfordshire, just short of Lyonsdown Road, and this was open for traffic on Saturday 4 August 1906. This was Bank Holiday weekend and over 38,000 people travelled on the trams. Amongst the passengers on the first tram was a Mrs Harper of Potters Road, New Barnet who had also ridden on the very first train to leave High Barnet Station on Monday 1 April 1872. Unfortunately, she did not have a memento of that particular journey as the Great Northern Railway made sure that they collected tickets from all their passengers.

In May 1906, Hertfordshire County Council had awarded a contract for the building of a line southwards from Barnet Church to meet the existing line at their boundary with Middlesex. After some delay this was duly completed and it was opened on Thursday 28 March 1907 at a cost of £22,000. Five new cars entered service and these carried the legend 'County Council of Hertfordshire' on their sides; all the other trams, of course, had 'County Council of Middlesex' on them. They were, however, all operated by MET and every tram carried 'Metropolitan Electric Tramways' on the lowermost panels, just above the wheels.

The coming of the trams to Barnet changed the town forever. In the Easter of 1907 the *Barnet Press* reported that there had never been such crowds on a public holiday and 'it looked as if Hampstead Heath and other notable spots northward had been deserted for the day.' The weather was glorious and the great majority of the visitors made for Hadley Woods and a multitude of children played on Hadley Green. Local estimates put the crowds at 10,000, although some of the London papers claimed there were as many as 50,000. Some of the citizens of Barnet may have looked on in horror at the invasion of their quiet rural retreat, but licensed victuallers and caterers were doubtless well pleased.

A vivid description of a tram ride was carried in the same issue of the paper, which gives an idea of how open the countryside then was:

> It is an interesting stretch of country from Willenhall to Barnet, with views magnificent. Looking to the right from the top of the car, the attention of the traveller is first directed to woody Greenhill Park, where an army of rooks are to be seen fighting over sticks with which to furnish their draughty apartments in the tree tops. There is a mansion in the Park hidden by the trees. Never seen it? That may be, but still there is a mansion there, and a fine old building, too. Numbered among the distinguished residents is L.G. Haslock, Esq., JP, chairman of the East Barnet District Council, who keeps in perfect order the body over which he presides. He also

keeps his weather eye on the County Council. To the left, dividing green and other fields is the Great Northern Railway, along which crawl, at stated intervals, trains, sometimes full, sometimes not, to and from London. In about the time it takes one to light his pipe, the car reaches the top of Station-road, the borderline dividing snobby Lyonsdown from Barnet with the pubs. If you like to get out here and climb a tree at the corner of Greenhill Park, you might be able on a sunny day to distinguish the East Barnet Public Offices from among the other palatial buildings at the bottom of Station-road. Look for a clock, and if you see one at the correct time depend upon it that is the one that adorns the Council Offices. There was a period in its history when the clock never did its duty properly, not even with the coaxing of experts with the best of machine oil and a barrowload of patent tools, but it goes A1 now. A swarthy amateur has taken it in hand, who eases the cog wheels with wagon grease, and pushes the hands ahead with a broomstick.

Passing from the top of Station-road, the next object of interest that merits attention is the arch at the bottom of Barnet Hill. Gentlemen are requested not to make any rude remarks, though a few oily drops of water descend from the railway on their toppers. Built in the early ages, this arch is much prized by residents as an object of historical interest, and but for the indignant protest of locals, the county authorities would have knocked it down without the slightest qualms of conscience. There is abundance of accommodation for the extra traffic. Two cars can pass under the arch comfortably. By way of providing entertainment for the other traffic during the passing of cars under the arch, the County Council have kindly arranged for nose bags for the horses, and for the supply of refreshments to the drivers thereof from a neighbouring coffee stall.

'A'-type car No.113 heads northwards up Archway Road on the service to Whetstone. The large hoarding on the left is advertising new houses on the Milton Park Estate, a few hundred yards further north on the right-hand side. (Commercial postcard)

The citizens of Barnet turn out in force for a ride on the new electric cars. On this postcard the inscription on the back read 'This is one of the new trams. Next time you come to Barnet you will be able to ride on one. They stop by Barnet Church.' This car had previously only operated as far as Whetstone, as the hastily improvised 'Barnet' indicator board shows. (Andrew Forsyth Collection)

Proceeding up Barnet Hill, you find on your right the Barnet coal depot with its picturesque sheds and stables, and, further on, Barnet railway station, lately altered to suit the convenience of travellers who like the cold east winds. Away behind the railway station stretch Hadley Woods, far famed for early cuckoos, loving couples, and spring poets. You will find the walk from this point to the Woods rather long. The usual route is by Hadley Church, and in case you are not versed in the customs of the port, it is as well to inform you that it is usual to sing loudly or yell "The Old Bull and Bush" as you pass from the Great North-road and across the green and into the common. The residents on the green are passionately fond of music.

But to return to Barnet Hill. A magnificent view of the whereabouts of Totteridge golf course may be obtained by standing and twisting your head southwards. That red roofed building you see half-hidden by trees is not the outhouse it looks at a distance. No, it is Totteridge Golf House. With a strong glass you may discover Harry Vardon surveying the scene from the terrace, and some duffers from Fleet-street footling approaches to the last green. By the time you have returned your seat and apologised for scraping your neighbour's patent boots with your hobnails, you have reached the terminus – Barnet Church – past which you are requested – should you continue the tour on a motor on Sunday – to go quietly, in other words, not to toot or tootle to the annoyance of worshippers. On the road to the left of the church there is situated the County Court Office, at which summonses for debts are issued at the rate of 500 a month, and by following the road on the right you proceed in the direction of the Town Hall (under new management), where once a month before the learned Registrar and His Honour the Judge, an exhibition is given of hopeful assets, in the shape of squalling babies. Having conducted the traveller from Willenhall to the very centre of the town, we leave him, trusting that his own good sense will dictate to him where to quench his thirst and that the star of fortune will guide him safely through the dangers of yawning drains, spotted fever, and two-ton motor cars.

The hum of the motors; the squealing of the wheels on bends; the rattling of the bodywork and the clanking noise of the wheels as they went over the gaps in the rails all contributed to the distinctive sound of the new form of transport. Passengers on the open-top decks of the tramcars, as well as feeling the wind in their faces, would hear the hissing, swooshing sound of the trolley wheel on the overhead wire. Negotiating ones way along the top deck of a moving tram was quite an art as it pitched and rolled its way through the suburbs.

Whilst this activity had been going on, the MET were busy expanding their network in other parts of North London. Back in 1904, they had opened lines from Finsbury Park to Wood Green (on 22 July) and on 20 August of that year lines from Manor House to Seven Sisters Corner and from Wood Green to Bruce Grove were opened. At the western end of their territory a line was opened from The Crown in Cricklewood to Church Lane Edgware on 3 December. They were also opening lines in the Edmonton area, but it is the Wood Green and Cricklewood lines that interest us most.

On Wednesday 28 November 1906, the Wood Green line was further extended as far as The Ranelagh in Bounds Green Road and six months later, on Friday 10 May 1907, a further extension opened, to New Southgate Station, then called New Southgate and Colney Hatch.

Whit Monday 1919 at Golders Green and a crowd waits optimistically to board a tram towards Whetstone. The gentleman carrying what appears to be a large table would not have been popular with the conductor or with the other passengers. (© TfL from the London Transport Museum Collection)

X-29. 20 M. 4/09.

... THE ...

Metropolitan Electric Tramways, Ltd.

NOTICE.

On and after THURSDAY, 8th APRIL, 1909,

A SERVICE OF ELECTRIC CARS WILL BE RUN AT FREQUENT INTERVALS
BETWEEN

NORTH FINCHLEY (Junction of Woodhouse Road and Great North Road),
and FINSBURY PARK,
Via NEW SOUTHGATE and WOOD GREEN.

FARES—either way between—

North Finchley & New Southgate Station " The Orange Tree " & "The Ranelagh " New Southgate Station & Lordship Lane " The Ranelagh " & Turnpike Lane ... Nightingale Road & " The Salisbury " ... Lordship Lane & Finsbury Park ...	**1d.**
North Finchley & Lordship Lane ... " The Orange Tree " & Turnpike Lane ... New Southgate Station & Finsbury Park	**2d.**
North Finchley & Finsbury Park ...	**3d.**

TRANSFER FARES.
Change Cars at Great North Road.
" The Orange Tree " & Squires Lane }
" The Orange Tree " & Tally Ho Corner } **1¼.**

WORKMEN'S FARES.
North Finchley & Lordship Lane ... **1d.**
Two-Journey Ticket ... ... **2¼.**
New Southgate Statn. & Finsbury Park **1d.**
Two-Journey Ticket ... ... **2¼.**

Children over **5** years of age charged Full Fare. All Children **under 5** occupying
Seats must be paid for.

	LEAVE WOODHOUSE ROAD.			LEAVE FINSBURY PARK.	
	Week-days.	Sundays.		Week-days.	Sundays.
First Car...	5.5 a.m.	9.6 a.m.	First Car...	5.53 a.m.	9.30 a.m.
Last Car ...	11.57 p.m.	11.33 p.m.	Last Car ...	11.49 p.m.	11.15 p.m.

WORKMEN'S CARS WILL RUN AS UNDER:—

Woodhouse Road Terminus.	New S'gate Station.	Wood Green.	FINSBURY PARK. arr.	dep.	Wood Green.	New S'gate Station.	Woodhouse Road Terminus.
5 5	5 17	5 32	5 51	—	5 48	6 3	6 15
5 25	5 37	5 52	6 11	—	6 4	6 19	6 31
5 41	5 53	6 8	6 27	5 53	6 12	6 27	6 39
5 57	6 9	6 24	6 43	—	6 24	6 39	6 51
—	—	6 32	6 51	6 13	6 32	6 47	6 59
6 13	6 25	6 40	6 59	—	6 40	6 55	7 7
6 21	6 33	6 48	7 7	6 29	6 48	7 3	7 15
6 29	6 41	6 56	7 15	—	6 56	7 11	7 23
6 37	6 49	7 4	7 23	6 45	7 4	7 19	7 31
6 45	6 57	7 12	7 31	6 53	7 12	7 27	7 39
*6 53	7 5	7 20	7 39	7 1	7 20	7 35	7 47
7 1	7 13	7 28	7 47	7 9	7 28	7 43	7 55
7 9	7 21	7 36	7 55	7 17	7 36	7 51	8 3
7 17	7 29	7 44	8 3	7 25	7 44	7 59	—
7 25	7 37	7 52	—	7 33	7 52	8 7	—
7 33	7 45	8 0	—	—	—	—	—

N.B.—Workmen's TWO-JOURNEY TICKETS are available for a second journey at
any time (Sundays, Good Friday, Christmas Day and Bank Holidays excep'ed).

Cars will stop to take up or let down Passengers at the specified **STOPPING
PLACES ONLY.**

Passengers will please notify the Conductor of their intention to alight **BEFORE**
reaching such **STOPPING PLACES,** and are cautioned against attempting to
enter or leave the Cars when in motion.

MANOR HOUSE OFFICES,
SEVEN SISTERS ROAD, FINSBURY PARK, N.
5th April, 1909.

By Order, W. E. HAMMOND,
Traffic Manager.

The photograph on this postcard from 1916 was obviously taken from the top of a tramcar and demonstrates the casual approach of other, horse-drawn, road users. Tram motormen would have had to have been very alert in order to avoid accidents. (Percy Reboul Collection)

For a short time single-deck trams of the kind being used on the route through Alexandra Palace were used, but these were soon replaced by double-deck cars. There was therefore a gap between New Southgate and North Finchley which had to be filled. Before this could happen, it was first necessary to widen Woodhouse Road to 60ft; a photograph taken at the turn of the century shows this to be nothing more than a country lane, complete with fields and a haystack – in fact it was called Woodhouse Lane.

Finchley Council undertook the work with a grant from the Middlesex County Council of £10,000. The missing section along Woodhouse Road and Friern Barnet Road was finally opened on Thursday 8 April 1909 and cars could run all the way from Tally Ho to Finsbury Park. There was, however, a pinch point at the bridge over the railway at New Southgate which was too narrow to take double tracks. Friern Barnet Council wanted the bridge widened but was reluctant to pay two thirds of the cost, which was what the MCC had demanded. It took a further four years for the dispute to be settled and the bridge was widened in 1913 and double tracks installed. Because of the shallow depth of the road it was not possible to erect the usual traction poles on the bridge itself so poles were erected at the ends, with a long span wire connecting them. This arrangement lasted until the trams and their successors, the trolleybuses, were withdrawn.

At the western end, the line from Golders Green to Tally Ho opened on Thursday 16 December 1909 and the tram routes for the area were complete. This route was particularly important because it provided a quick and convenient link with the nearest Underground

C/1-type car No.198 heads down Wood Green High Road towards Finsbury Park. As well as the destination roller blind, it also carries a circular metal plate with the letter F, the code for the North Finchley–Finsbury Park service. (Andrew Forsyth Collection)

station at Golders Green. This was the northern terminus of the Charing Cross, Edgware and Hampstead Railway (later to be renamed the Northern Line) which had opened on Saturday 22 June 1907. This line was not extended to Hendon Central until Monday 19 November 1923, thence to Edgware on Monday 18 August 1924, so the trams provided a valuable service for some fifteen years. The MET and the railway company cooperated in providing through ticketing, so passengers could buy a ticket on the tram which would take them right into town by tube.

The other link to the Underground network was the tram route to Finsbury Park (later numbered 21). This was so heavily used that, in the 1920s in particular, long queues were the order of the day and police were sometimes called out to control the crowds at Finsbury Park. It was not until 1932 and 1933 when the Piccadilly Line was extended northwards to Cockfosters that relief came. The situation could have been a lot easier but the London & North Eastern Railway (LNER), and its predecessor the Great Northern Railway (GNR), not only consistently refused to electrify or upgrade its service but also opposed the extension of the Piccadilly Line. The GNR considered that freight traffic (particularly the carriage of coal from the north) was more important to them than mere commuters. The LNER themselves calculated that electrification would more than double the level of service but the investment was not forthcoming and it was only just before the formation of the London Transport Passenger Board (LPTB) in 1933 that they made any concerted effort to apply for Government funding, which was refused. The North London Travelling Facilities Committee, a local pressure group, called for an improved service on the High Barnet branch of the LNER where it complained that the trains were infrequent, unpunctual and often lacked heating facilities. In 1927 it pointed out that in the evening peak hours twenty-two trains from Moorgate Street went to New Barnet, sixteen to Alexandra Palace and only fourteen to High Barnet. It commented that public transport in the Tally Ho area was particularly unsatisfactory and called for an extension of the Piccadilly Line northwards, with a possible station at Tally Ho. Like the proposals in the 1940s to electrify the GNR line to Alexandra Palace via Muswell Hill it came to nothing, but it is interesting to speculate the effect on these two areas that tube stations would have had.

The coming of the trams led to the development of the area. New shopping parades were built at both ends of Woodhouse Road in 1910 and new houses were soon being built.

This photograph, which was taken on 29 April 1930, highlights the problems at Finsbury Park with trams, buses, cars and pedestrians all sharing the same road space. (©TfL from the London Transport Museum Collection)

Although the Feltham trams carried more people, the fact that that they had sliding doors meant that passengers had to wait until these were opened before they could board. This scene was at Finsbury Park on 31 May 1933. (© TfL from the London Transport Museum Collection)

In 1901 the population of Finchley and Friern Barnet was 33,692; ten years later it had risen to 64,091 – a huge 90 per cent increase. Amongst the many beneficiaries of the trams were the shops in Wood Green, which now became easily accessible to residents of Friern Barnet and New Southgate. At the northern end of the line, the countryside around Barnet became a magnet at weekends and on public holidays. Visitors to Barnet Market could now be carried right to the top of Barnet Hill, rather than having to walk up from the station.

During seven days in August 1922 a traffic survey was carried out at Barnet Hill which gives an interesting picture of traffic conditions at the time. Of a total of 42,940 vehicles counted, 51 per cent (21,728) were motor vehicles (including twenty-five traction engines); 32 per cent (13,749) were cycles and over 11 per cent (4,875) were horse-drawn. Tramcars accounted for some 5 per cent (2,242), omnibuses 2 per cent (930) and there were 177 cattle, sheep and pigs.

CHAPTER 4

How They Worked

The very first tramcars, known as 'B'-type, had open-top decks, with ornate iron scrollwork along the sides; the lower decks had windows and longitudinal seats. There were stairs at both ends of the cars and the trams could be driven from either end. The early cars of 'A'-type carried a large headlight above the driver; this was subsequently moved down to the dash panel in front of the driver in later types. The cars were painted in signal red and ivory, a livery they carried until they were taken over by LPTB in July 1933, after which they were repainted into standard LT red and cream.

It is not difficult to imagine the impression the trams would have made on the streets – each car was just over 34ft in length, 11ft high and 7ft wide, about twice the size of a motor bus of the period. When comparison is made with the standard Routemaster bus (approx 27ft 6in long, 14ft 6in high and 7ft 11in wide), which was to come into service 54 years later, it is no wonder the trams were considered the last word in public transport. As we have seen, there were comparatively few homes with electricity in 1905, so a brightly lit tramcar might well have been most people's first encounter with the wonders of electricity. Later versions of the tramcars had balconies which extended over the drivers positions at each end which raised their capacity to seventy. Covered tops were first introduced around 1908 but did not become general until around 1929 when a tramcar modernisation programme was nearing completion.

Because trams were capable of being driven from either end, they did not have to be turned round at the terminus. The motorman simply removed the handle from the controller at one end and walked through the car and inserted the handle on the controller at the other end.

There were eight notches on the controller; on the first four the motors were connected in series, which gave gradual acceleration, and on the last four the motors were connected in parallel, which gave increased speed. For normal continuous running only the fourth and eighth notches were used, the others being for acceleration only. Turning the handle in an anti-clockwise direction progressively activated the electric brakes on the wheels. The current for this was obtained not from the overhead power supply but from the motors, which meant that the faster the tram was travelling the more braking power was available. Thus, if the tram was travelling at speed, the braking would start on selection of the seventh notch; if it was travelling slowly braking would not start until the fourth or fifth notches were selected. Once the tram had come to a stop the handbrake was applied; this was operated by a large wheel next to the controller. The magnetic track brake, or 'maggie' in motorman's parlance, clamped a brake shoe directly onto the track. When weather conditions made the track slippery, or in the autumn when there was a build-up of leaves, adhesion would be greatly reduced and sand would be distributed on the track by a pipe which led from a sand hopper located under the seats in the downstairs saloon and which was operated by means of a foot pedal operated by the motorman. The trams averaged a speed of 10.5mph although they could reach 20mph on long straight stretches. Apart from the familiar noise of the electric motors, the rattle of the bodywork and the sound of the wheels on the rails, the most distinctive sound was of the warning gong which the motorman controlled through a foot pedal. This was so loud that they were instructed not to use it outside churches and other places of worship during the hours when services were taking place. The tram bodies were mounted on two bogies, called trucks, each of which had four wheels. The outermost pair of wheels on each truck was powered by a motor, while the innermost pair of wheels were unpowered and were of smaller diameter; these were known as pony wheels.

Above left: The business end of a tram with the controller and the toothed wheel and its 'dog' with which the motorman released the handbrake by using his foot. (Author)

Above right: At the terminus, the conductor would walk through the car and reverse all the seat backs ready for the return journey. (Author)

Right: Stray dogs would be deposited unharmed on to a tray just ahead of the front wheels, thanks to the hinged 'cowcatcher'. (Author)

The overhead wires were divided into sections about half a mile in length and each section was controlled by a circuit cabinet on the pavement. In the event of a problem a section could then be isolated and the power switched off so that repairs could be made. Between each section was a short stretch of 'dead' wire and motormen had to ease off the controller at these points to prevent a dewirement. The trams did not carry speedometers so motormen learned to judge their speed by the time taken between each section and were thus able to keep to schedule. At the end of each journey, the conductor would grab a lanyard connected to the trolley pole and, walking round the tram, reconnect the pole on to the overhead wire so that it was facing in the opposite direction. The tension on the arm was sufficient to keep the wheel in contact with the wire yet flexible enough to negotiate junctions where wires crossed. At junctions where several tram routes converged, pointsmen were stationed whose sole job was to operate a large lever in the pavement which controlled the points. These men had to be on station throughout the hours of tram operation and regardless of the weather conditions and in later years they were afforded some protection from the elements by small canvas huts, but it was still an unpleasant and boring job.

At first the trams carried no route numbers; roller blinds at the front and rear showed their final destination. Boards at the side between decks carried the ultimate destinations and an intermediate point thus: WHETSTONE, FINCHLEY, HIGHGATE. Within a couple of years, circular metal plates were installed on the front of the cars above the driver's position. Cars bound for Barnet carried white discs with a red letter B surrounded by a red circle; North Finchley cars had a white disc with a blue rim and with the letter F in the centre; Whetstone cars had white triangle on a red circle with the letter W. Route numbers were subsequently introduced around 1914. It is possible that this simple recognition system was employed because of the number of illiterate people who were unable to read the destination indicators.

Initially the only real competition to the trams was the horse bus which suffered from being small (it could only carry around twenty-six passengers) and was relatively expensive to run: each bus required about ten horses which had to be stabled and fed, and the price of oats was continually increasing. In those days many people started work at 7a.m. and the provision of a reliable, cheap and frequent (about every six minutes) means of getting to work was of great benefit. Horse buses did not usually start operating until about 7a.m. so they were not much use to working men. By contrast, the trams were large (approximately seventy seats), smooth, and operated from the early hours, with special fares for workmen.

Although the LCC lines between Archway Bridge and Archway Tavern had been electrified in December 1905, through running by LCC and MET, cars did not become possible until Thursday 24 September 1914 when a change pit was installed. This was necessary because of the fundamental difference between the two systems. When they started to consider electrification of their tramways, the LCC had initially opted for a conduit system which entailed the installation of a slot between the rails into which a plough underneath the tramcars fitted and which picked up the current from buried electrified rails. The system was less obtrusive since it did not require the use of overhead wires, but it was considerably more expensive and was not taken up by other tramway operators and, in fact, the LCC later utilised the overhead system on certain of their lines. In order for trams to run on both systems, LCC cars had to be fitted with overhead booms and the MET cars with carriers for a plough. At the Archway Tavern change pit, an MET car arriving from the north would have its boom lowered and a waiting plough would be inserted into the carrier under the car by means of a metal fork, the tram would then proceed on LCC lines to its destination. The system was of course reversed for trams heading beyond Archway to Whetstone.

In practice, both LCC and MET cars operated the service, with the fares generated being allocated between the two companies. It was easy to distinguish between MET and LCC cars as the latter were painted in the company's chocolate-brown livery (officially called Crimson Lake) until 1927, after which they were repainted in vermilion and primrose yellow.

Unfortunately, the tickets on both systems, which were of the Bell Punch type, were not compatible: an LCC 1 penny ticket was blue while an MET 1*d* ticket was white which must, initially at least, have lead to some confusion amongst both staff and passengers. Fares were based on the rate of 1*d* per mile but the rate for workmen was only ½*d*. All London tramway companies had, by law, to offer special reduced rates for workers travelling before 8a.m.; such concessions were not, however, made mandatory on buses, which was a source of some grievance to the tramway companies, as they felt it was unfairly penalising them. With their obligation to maintain part of the road surface, and the cost of maintaining track, wires and electricity supplies as well, it can be seen that it was difficult to make a reasonable profit and this lead eventually to a decline in standards in later years.

The MCC were responsible for the initial construction of the lines and alterations to the road infrastructure and they built Finchley depot and the adjacent substation. The MET provided the trams and were legally responsible for the upkeep of the road not only between the tramlines but also 18in each side and wooden blocks were used to achieve a smooth surface. The MCC had originally wanted to use granite setts but there were letters of complaint from members of the public to Finchley Council. North Ward Residents' Association submitted a petition stating 'it would be extremely detrimental to the district of Finchley and a source of great annoyance to the residents and users of the thoroughfares.' West Finchley Ratepayers said 'it would seriously depreciate the value of the property.' In the end the Board of Trade held an enquiry and found in favour of the council and wooden blocks were installed at a cost of 13*s* per square yard, the total cost amounting to over £43,000; the blocks were then sprayed with tar which gave a very smooth surface. When the wood blocks were subsequently removed they were eagerly seized by local residents as they made excellent fuel for the open fires that everyone had then. The only drawback was that small stones which had accumulated over the years would explode from the grate with some force! As a result of the track-laying, on many roads the central section was in much better condition than the rest, as local authorities had still not replaced the dusty, uneven surface that had been there for years and which had only had to bear horse-drawn traffic. Eventually Finchley and Friern Barnet Councils got round to making good the haunches with tarmac to the benefit of all road users.

With the installation of tramlines in the centre of roads it became necessary to widen highways. The MCC wanted to widen Woodhouse Lane to 45ft but Finchley UDC insisted on 60ft. In the minutes of Christ Church, Friern Barnet Road dated 27 October 1902 it was recorded:

At the Archway change pit the plough is about to be inserted under London Transport H1-type car No.872. (D.W.K. Jones)

The Tramways Company had obtained powers for the compulsory acquisition of land for the widening of Friern Barnet Road and had undertaken to pave with wood blocks the whole of the road in front of the church. The Light Railway Commission had decided that the roadway must be 50ft and that it be widened on the north side.

We thus have the advent of trams to thank for much our modern road structure. Initially, the poles supporting the overhead wires were erected down the centre of the roads and they bore an ornate bracket on either side that held the wires, but the poles proved to be a hazard to traffic and were subsequently replaced by March 1913 with poles on the pavements which had carrier wires from one side of the road to the other from which the electric wires were strung. This change has proved to be a valuable guide to historians in dating otherwise undated photographs from the period.

At North Finchley, trams terminated either side of the Park Road Hotel, which would subsequently be demolished in 1927 and a new pub, the Tally Ho, built on the site. Trams coming from Golders Green reversed in Ballards Lane, while those from Highgate reversed in the High Road, outside number 740. Trams terminating at Whetstone did so outside The Green Man, and the terminus at Barnet was just south of the church.

MET uniforms consisted of dark blue jackets and trousers with a thin red piping and the caps also had red piping, together with a badge containing the MET logo - a magnet and wheel. The uniform remained much the same until the demise of the trams, although when MET became part of the Underground group their logo, the familiar circle and bar, bore the word TRAMWAYS. During the First World War, many MET men were enlisted into the army and women were employed as conductors. Their uniform consisted of a jacket and long skirt with black boots together with a wide-brimmed hat. Although the women were subsequently dismissed when the war ended, they had proved their competence, willingness and ability and it was their work on the tramways and in other industries that led to their acceptance in a male-dominated society and resulted in their getting the vote in February 1918, albeit only for those over thirty; full emancipation did not come until March 1928.

'A'-type car No.75 on route 46 is about to head down Ballards Lane to Golders Green. Although this photograph is undated, it had to have been taken before May 1926 because from that date the practice of giving short journeys between North Finchley and Golders Green a separate number was discontinued. Thereafter all journeys came under route 40. (Commercial postcard)

The newly installed poles must have caused some consternation to residents of these houses in High Road, Whetstone. (London Borough of Barnet Archives)

The First World War saw the fixing of air-raid alarms to the traction poles and these were doubtless in use when a famous event occurred. Starting in 1915, London had been the victim of several Zeppelin raids but as air defences improved, the raiders did not continue to have it all their own way and on Saturday 2 September 1916 German airship number SL11 was forced down over Cuffley. Three weeks later, on the night of Sunday 1 October, airship L31, piloted by the notorious (in British eyes, anyway) Kapitan Heinrich Mathy, was to suffer a similar fate. Planes were sent up to intercept the Zeppelin, including a BE 2C biplane based at Hornchurch and piloted by Lieutenant Wulstan Tempest. Although he had been instructed not to climb higher than 8,000ft, when he saw the Zeppelin caught in the searchlights at Barnet he climbed to 15,000ft and managed to fire off several rounds from his Lewis gun into the L31, which burst into flames and crashed at Oakmere Farm in Potters Bar, killing all twenty crew on board. The story goes that Tempest then landed at North Weald, overturning his plane as he did so, hitched a ride on a motorbike and sidecar and returned to his friends where he finished his dinner. He was subsequently awarded the DSO for his bravery. On that night there was a specially equipped tram, painted in dark green and with a searchlight mounted on it, parked at Barnet Church. It was almost certainly partly responsible for illuminating the ill-fated Zeppelin.

Four years after the end of the war, on Sunday 7 August 1922, a white marble tablet was unveiled at Finchley depot in memory of eighteen men from the depot who lost their lives in the service of King and country. A service was conducted by the Revd F.S. Lee from Christ Church, North Finchley and assisted by the Revds L.J. McCrea from North Finchley Congregational Church and J. Cleal of North Finchley Baptist Church.

Track maintenance was, of course, a vital part of tramway operations and perhaps the most dramatic was the rail grinding machine which was a converted single-deck tramcar that had a large grinding wheel underneath that would smooth off the rails. The noise, dust and sparks created can be imagined. One resident also recalls an occasion when, walking to school one morning, he came across linesmen working on the track on the railway bridge in Friern Barnet Road. They had just cut out an oblong hole an inch wide with an oxy-acetylene torch in order to bolt a new rail to the old one and he picked up the still-hot piece of metal as a souvenir, much to the amusement of the workmen. Nevertheless, he took it home, painted it gold and kept it as a talisman for many years. In an incident in January 1935, a flash of lightning struck the overhead wires near to Cornwall Avenue in Ballards Lane and broke the span wires by fusing them, so that the power wire hung down to within 6ft of the road. Fortunately, a passing motorist gave the alarm and a crew from Finchley depot were there within minutes and effected repairs so that the service was not interrupted for too long.

Whilst the trams ruled the roads for a few years, there was a development that would eventually offer them real competition: the motor bus. In March 1905 the unladen weight for motor vehicles had been increased to 5 tons and the width from 6ft 6in to 7ft 2in but the solid tyres gave a very harsh ride on the poorly maintained roads and they were mechanically unreliable until the London General Omnibus Co. (LGOC) introduced the 'B'-type bus in 1910. Over 6,800 were produced and some even shipped over to France to act as troop transports in the war. They lasted until 1926 but in the meantime several improved vehicle types were being introduced: the 'K'-type in 1919; 'S'-type in 1920 and 'NS'-type in 1923.

When the 'LT'-type entered service in 1929 it introduced completely new standards of comfort. It had a diesel engine, pneumatic tyres, a covered top deck, upholstered seats and a capacity of fifty-six. In addition, buses could and did stop anywhere (fixed bus stops were not introduced in London until 1935) but trams had fixed stopping places. Suddenly the trams looked very dated and their inflexibility and the high costs of maintaining the infrastructure to support them (track, overhead and generating capacity) led the authorities to start contemplating their eventual replacement with something more modern.

In his book *LCC Electric Tramways*, Robert J. Harley makes a very interesting point that is not, perhaps, realised today: in the early years of the century, people smelt rather unpleasant:

> Poverty played a huge role, and many London families did not have access to a bath or adequate washing facilities. Workmen's clothing was made to last and would often remain soiled for weeks. Ladies of a certain class did use perfume, lavender water or eau de cologne, but most folk did without.

Of course, in those days, most men smoked, and pipes in particular were common. An upper deck of a tram would have been extremely unhealthy, particularly after covered tops were introduced. Only the bravest of women would venture on to the top deck as, apart from the difficulty of climbing stairs in voluminous skirts, there was the added peril of gentlemen catching glimpses of their ankles. Notices inside the trams carried the warning: 'No Hawking. No Spitting.' Hawking, in this case, did not refer to selling things.

The first 150 examples of 'LT'-type buses had open staircases but the remaining 1,077 would be enclosed, offering even more comfort. (© TfL from the London Transport Museum Collection)

An interesting line-up in Finchley depot in March 1938. On the left is a snowbroom which was used to clear the rails in winter, while cars Nos 2202 and 2250 are former MET 'H'-type cars which were renumbered by LPTB in 1933. (Andrew Forsyth Collection)

From the very first, one of the features of the tram services, and the thing that made them very popular with the working classes, was the running of the early morning workmen's services at reduced fares. The first trams would be on the streets soon after 5a.m. and, for those wishing to spend a night in town, the last northbound trams did not leave the West End until some 15 minutes before midnight. On the occasion of the Coronation of King George VI, London Transport organised all-night bus services on a handful of routes on the night of Tuesday 11 May–Wednesday 12 May. Trams on services 19 (Barnet – Tottenham Court Road) and 21 (North Finchley – Holborn) started earlier than normal, with the first ones arriving in London around 4a.m. on the Wednesday.

CHAPTER 5

THE BUS PIRATES

In 1912 MET, together with the LGOC, LUT and some bus operators, had become part of the Underground Electric Railways Ltd group (UERL), which became known as the Combine. By this time the MET was carrying 1,727,000 passengers a week and taking £8,589 in revenue, so it was now well established. The period immediately after the awful First World War saw a new generation of men and women who now expected more from life; after all, they had been promised 'a land fit for heroes'. Despite most of these promises being unfulfilled, some things did get better; in particular there was an increase in leisure facilities. Greyhound racing was introduced and football became hugely popular (Wembley Stadium opened in 1923). Railway companies brought in Day Trip tickets and charabancs were introduced which made trips to the country and seaside easy and more affordable.

Unfortunately, the increasing demand for public transport went hand-in-hand with a reduction in supply. The number of buses in London had dropped from just over 4,000 before the war to barely half that number after (apart from the loss due to mechanical failures and ageing vehicles, over 950 'B'-type buses had been sent to France and Belgium as troop transports during the war). Travelling conditions became intolerable and queues became longer. The General were even forced to convert over 100 lorries to carry passengers and, needless to say, these were not well received by passengers used to rather more comfortable means of transport. On the technical side, an agreement between LGOC and the Associated Equipment Company (AEC), a fellow member of the Combine, meant that new General buses were mainly built by AEC, and companies such as Leyland, Dennis and Straker Squire were unable to gain a foothold in the London market.

The constituent companies of the Combine had an agreement between themselves that in order to protect the viability of the trams they would keep the operation of motor buses on tram routes to a minimum. Strange as it may seem, there was actually nothing preventing other operators of buses setting up in competition to the General; it appears that it never dawned on anyone to actually do it. Providing that a bus passed the stringent Metropolitan Police tests for roadworthiness, they would have no objection to such services being run.

By the 1920s, public disquiet became more vocal and the Combine became to be looked upon as an uncaring, inefficient monopoly, although in fact it never had monopoly powers. Into this unsatisfactory situation a hero emerged. A taxi driver, Arthur George Partridge, had often seen long queues for buses as he drove around London and he decided to explore the possibility of starting his own bus service. Having got financial backing from two colleagues, he approached Leyland who were more than willing to give him favourable terms for the purchase of one of their LB models for £1,600. The bus was passed by the police and at noon on Saturday 5 August 1922 the vehicle, with natty white sidewall tyres and in handsome brown and cream livery that distinguished it from the red General buses and trams, entered service on route 11. The General had got wind of this new service and had made plans accordingly; they had four of their own buses shadowing the *Chocolate Express*, as it came to be called, and did everything they could to prevent customers from using it. This situation continued for some days until an article on the service in the *Daily Herald* roused public anger that the efforts of a small entrepreneur were being sabotaged by an organisation that had failed to deliver acceptable services themselves. The Combine backed down and the stage was set for a fascinating period in London's transport history.

Before long other independent operators, most of them one-man outfits, and often ex-servicemen with gratuities, were able to offer competition to the Combine on the busiest routes and then only at peak hours. In March 1923 a group of ex-servicemen started a motor bus service between Tally Ho and Golders Green and appropriately named it the X Service. The bus would follow some distance behind a tram car and pick up those who had unfortunately been unable to get on board. The service operated throughout the rush hours and was welcomed by many passengers, as can be seen by this letter in the *Finchley Press* in April 1923:

Will you please allow me space to comment on the unjust opposition of the omnibus combine against any small men who put buses on the streets of London and suburbs? Some of these men are ex-service men and have invested all their money in vehicles. As soon as they are on the road they are chased, and their livelihood jeopardised by the Combine. Look at the "Admiral" buses, how they are interfered with on the Southgate route; and again with the 'ex-Service bus' to North Finchley. When the public wanted better services to Finchley from Golders Green, the Combine did nothing. Then, as soon as fresh enterprise appears its vehicles are opposed by a Combine service. It is time that this matter was dealt with by fresh laws, as the small owner has an equal right to the streets with the larger concerns. Trusting that this appeal for the small man will help him in his fight to live.

The writer did not give his name, but signed himself 'Unfair Opposition', so it is possible that he had an axe to grind, and may even have been a bus proprietor; nevertheless the points that he made were valid ones.

A letter from the proprietor of Barnet Motor Services on 23 April 1923 said:

I wish to thank 'Over Sixty' for his suggestion with reference to extending the bus service now in operation between East Barnet and Hadley Highstone to Oakleigh Park Station. Unfortunately we have only the one bus at present, and this extension would mean that the complete journey could not be covered in one hour. Hence, there would necessarily be fewer journeys in the course of a day. Our original intention was to commence at Oakleigh Park, but the route had to be curtailed for the reasons stated. If circumstances should warrant the extension and evidence of a sufficient demand should be forthcoming, it is possible that your correspondent's suggestion may be favourably considered later.

MR. WARD'S
HENDON AND REGENT CIRCUS
OMNIBUS
IS NOW RUNNING AS UNDER :—

Hendon (Post Office).		Welsh Harp.		Cricklewood.	
9.0	a.m.	9.15	a.m.	9.25	a.m.
12.0	noon.	12.15	p.m.	12.25	p.m.
3.30	p.m.	3.45	,,	3.55	,,
6.30	,,	6.45	,,	6.55	,,

L E A V E S

Regent Circus. (Oxford Street).		Praed Street (Corner of).		Kilburn	
10.50	a.m.	10.45	a.m.	11.0	a.m.
2.0	p.m.	2.15	p.m.	2.30	p.m.
5.0	,,	5.15	,,	5.30	
8.0	,,	8.15	,,	8.30	

SUNDAYS.

LEAVES Post Office, Hendon.		LEAVES Regent Circus.	
9.0	a.m.	10.30	a.m.
2.0	p.m.	3.30	p.m.
7.0	p.m.	8.30	p.m.

Not all Pirate buses offered frequent services. (Author)

A local resident, Mr Alf Matthews, described a journey on one of the independents:

My first recollections go back to 1924, when I travelled daily from the top of Russell Lane to New Southgate Station on my way to town, dressed in the regulation bowler, striped trousers and, of course, a rolled-up umbrella. One morning I remember very vividly – we were a group of about a dozen people waiting patiently at first, but soon fretfully and anxiously – as the minutes were shortening to zero-time for our train. Still no bus, then we espied the 14-seater Fiat coming from Wood Green en route to Totteridge Church. Without further ado we surrounded it, the driver, who at first was somewhat taken aback with our request:'Go on, be a sport and run us to the station' called out the conductor. 'Ask the old chap (the only passenger) if he would like an extra ride?' All was well. After quickly turning round we piled in. That journey down Oakleigh Road must have broken the world record for all time – for the 'mile-and-a-half bus run.' As we drew up – right into the station forecourt- with such suddenness that we were nearly hurled out, a porter yelled 'Hold it, here they come.' For such was the friendly co-operation between passengers and bus and railway staff, that the train had actually been held up for us for nearly two minutes and was just on the move when we turned up!

Whilst the arrival of competition to the Combine was welcomed by the public, the haphazard operation of many of the services caused consternation to the authorities. The habit of some small operators of cherry picking the most profitable routes to operate on lead to unsafe practices like exceeding speed limits and vehicles cutting each other up. It was these tactics that resulted in them earning the nickname of 'pirates'. Some operators did not even bother with regular schedules; they might operate a vehicle on one route in the morning and then switch it to another route later in the day without, of course, warning the public. There were even reports of buses offloading passengers short of their destination so that the vehicle could turn round and go the other way, where crowds were greater and more fares could be gathered. So catching a bus became a hit and miss affair and early public enthusiasm turned to disappointment. One Finchley resident reported that although travellers in Whetstone had the benefit of a bus every minute, these were often overcrowded and buses built to carry fourteen might well carry forty. Because the job of collecting tickets was so difficult, apparently one conductor had an arrangement with the proprietor that he would guarantee to hand over £10 a day, and anything above that he would keep. A bus driver was convicted and fined 40s for driving at 20mph in Oakleigh Road, Whetstone, where the speed limit was 12mph. When stopped he said: 'What, again?' and was told that if he appeared before the court again his licence would be surrendered. Oakleigh Road was a particular haunt of the pirates who were keen to pick up the many workers at the Standard Telephones & Cables factory.

An indication of the nature of the independents' operations can be gleaned from their appearance on local routes. The 526D (North Finchley Swan & Pyramids to Wandsworth Bridge) was introduced by Birch Brothers in April 1925 and had had no fewer than sixteen independents running buses, although not all at the same time, whilst route 551 (Whetstone The Griffin to the Sparklets Works at Edmonton) had nine independent operators at one time or another.

At their height there were as many as 196 independents in London, and by 1926 they were operating over 670 buses, but some of these only operated on the busiest routes, and then only at peak hours. To make matters worse for the public, all London's tram men went on a nine-day strike on Saturday 22 March 1924 in pursuit of an 8s rise in wages and they were supported by busmen from the LGOC. Needless to say, the independent bus operators, which did not employ union men, continued working throughout the strike, thus enhancing their popularity with the public.

The country elected its first ever Labour Government in January 1924 and one of its early pieces of legislation was the London Traffic Act which came into effect on 1 October. In order to try and bring some semblance of order into the chaotic situation on London's streets the Act made it compulsory for bus operators to lodge proper schedules and timetables (which had to include regular services throughout the day during weekdays) with the Metropolitan Police. The Act actually made it a criminal offence not only to run a service that did not comply with the schedules and timetables, but also an offence *not* to run a service where details had been lodged. Powers were also given to the Ministry of Transport to introduce what were called 'Restricted Streets' where only a limited number of buses could operate. These restricted streets were mainly those on which trams operated but independent bus operators managed to get round these restrictions by introducing through routes which shadowed the trams for part of the route but would then go on

Three of the operators on route 551 (The Griffin, Whetstone – Sparklets Works, Edmonton). Dennises from Uneedus and Biss Brothers and a Leyland Lion PLSC from Prince. (Ron Kingdon Collection)

to serve destinations beyond the tram route. In the MET area bus route 284a, Victoria Station to North Finchley (extended to Hatfield in the summer) was introduced by Overground in 1925 and was subsequently taken over by LGOC; this was to become route 134 in 1930.

An interesting meeting took place in April 1926 between members of the Friern Barnet Urban District Council and two members of London Omnibus Proprietors Ltd, Messrs Walter J. Dangerfield and Dobbs, plus a representative of the MCC Light Railways Sub-Committee, Mr Pinching. Dangerfield and Dobbs urged the council to protest against any curtailment in omnibus travelling facilities in the Metropolitan area and also to support a petition which had been signed by over one million Londoners. Pinching addressed the Committee to the effect of unlimited omnibus traffic upon tramway services. The Committee were obviously won over by the omnibus men as they issued the following:

> That it is desirable in the interests of the inhabitants of the Urban District that there should be no restrictions placed on the travelling facilities afforded both by motor omnibuses and tramways and that an intimation to this effect be forwarded to the Ministry of Transport, the Member of Parliament for the Division , the Association of Omnibus Proprietors Ltd, the London General Omnibus Company Ltd and the Chairman of the Light Railways Sub-Committee of the County Council.

If Dangerfield and Dobbs could spare time to canvas a relatively small UDC such as Friern Barnet, it is fair to assume that they were doing the rounds of many other local authorities in London in an attempt to drum up support.

During the General Strike in May 1926 the independents continued to operate services with, in some cases, the owners themselves driving buses. As support for the strike was solid amongst other bus workers and their colleagues on the trams, the independents were continuing to offer the travelling public a choice and this enhanced their reputation. The appreciation of the role of independents was summed up in the report of the Annual General Meeting of Dennis Bros Ltd, vehicle manufacturers, in 1926:

> In recent months the number of independent buses has been considerably reduced by absorption into the Combine. This process may continue but it will be a sorry day if the sense of protection which a monopoly gives engenders in those who control London bus services a spirit of indifference to progress and improvement of which competition is the very breath of being.

After a time, things settled down and the independents started to introduce new routes not previously covered by either the trams or by General buses. This had the effect of widening the bus network, particularly in outlying areas. Eventually the LGOC started to buy up the independent companies and absorb them into their network and by the time of the creation of the London Passenger Transport Board (LPTB) on 1 July 1933 there were only fifty-one of them left, operating 258 buses. The LPTB became responsible for operating all buses and trams in London, as well as Underground trains, so the day of pirate buses and individual tram operators came to an end.

Ex–LCC E1 tram No.1622 and experimental Feltham car No.331 (*Cissie*) photographed at the National Tramway Museum. (Author)

The magnetic track brake sits between the wheels of *Cissie*. The wheels of the truck are all motored and are of equal size, which made it possible to lower the height of the tram. (Author)

CHAPTER 6

TRAM DEVELOPMENTS

With the improvements in motor omnibuses and competition from the pirate buses, tram operators in London lost ground to their rivals and fare revenues began to decline and the tram, which had once seemed so modern, now appeared very dated. The MET, in common with many other operators, embarked upon a programme of vehicle modernisation which largely consisted of putting roofs on their twenty-year-old open-top tramcars. This programme took place between 1928 and 1929 but the trams still looked their age and were not very passenger-friendly.

Both the LCC and the MET decided to develop a new generation of tramcar and produced experimental models to test out new ideas. In the case of the MET the new product, which cost £3,520, was a totally enclosed vehicle which, although it was some 2ft longer than existing cars, was some 4 tons lighter due to different methods of construction. It had more powerful motors and air brakes which contributed to a higher average speed of 12mph. It had platform doors at the front and back and could carry seventy-one passengers. The driver did not have to stand out in the open but regulations still did not allow windscreens to be fitted so his position was still a draughty one. Passengers now had the benefit of fully upholstered seats in the lower saloon and leatherette seats on the top deck, a great improvement on the slatted wooden seats of the older cars. The floors were grey rubber and passengers entered the car via only a single step. Electric bell pushes replaced the familiar bell cord and steps folded away when the car was in motion. The vehicle was painted in a light blue livery and carried hand-painted advertisements on each side for Palmolive. As soon as car No.318 entered service on Wednesday 30 March 1927 on route 40 from Barnet to Cricklewood it became known as *Bluebell*, a name which stuck. At the press launch at Hendon depot on 2 March 1927 Mr C.J. Spencer, the General Manager of MET, said the new trams would be more comfortable to ride in owing to their smooth running and the absence of rolling and pitching. He acknowledged the competition between the Combine's buses and trams but said there was room for both forms of transport.

Unfortunately *Bluebell* was to be involved in a fatal crash on the morning of Friday 17 June. The car had left the Barnet terminus at 7.21a.m. and, with some twelve passengers on board, started descending Barnet Hill at a sedate 5 or 6mph. The car was coasting and appeared to be fully in control but it carried on down the hill and struck the rear of a six-wheel Scammell lorry which was involved with roadworks at the foot of the hill. Impact speed was about 10mph and the lorry was pushed forward about 6ft. The front part of *Bluebell* was pushed in and the driver, Maurice Sidney Kent, was injured. He was taken to Victoria Cottage Hospital where

The new *Bluebell* at Finchley depot. (© TfL from the London Transport Museum Collection)

he was operated on for a compound fracture of the leg and was recovering from the anaesthetic when he had a sudden relapse and died from shock somewhere around 2.15p.m. His wife had gone to the hospital in the morning but was unable to see him and when she returned at 2.30p.m. she was given the sad news.

Maurice Kent's brother Edgar was the conductor of *Bluebell* on the day of the accident and he gave evidence at the inquest that *Bluebell* had suffered brake failure on a couple of previous occasions. In one incident the car had difficulty stopping on a slight incline in Regent's Park Road and when it eventually did so the passengers were removed and the car was taken out of service while repairs were made. He said his brother, who was forty-one, had been driving for fifteen years and was very careful. He said that both he and his brother had asked to be taken off *Bluebell* as it was causing them too much worry, mainly because they did not know it like the old cars, which they knew inside out. He said, 'We didn't know the new machine. It has never been pointed out to us.' This seems to be an extraordinary claim; if it was true it shows extreme laxity on the part of MET. When the car was returned to Finchley depot it was examined but no fault was found with the brakes. The tracks were inspected and sand was found for some 65 yards before the collision indicating that the brakes were being applied correctly. The exact cause of the accident was never discovered but the Metropolitan Police insisted that magnetic track brakes were added. The funeral of Maurice Kent took place on Thursday 7 July 1927. Over 200 MET employees assembled outside his house in Ingleway, North Finchley, and the coffin was carried by six tram men. At the junction of Crescent Way the MET band joined the procession, which made its way via Woodhouse Road, the Great North Road, Old Nether Street and Ballards Lane to the tram depot at Rosemont Avenue where there were dense crowds. The procession halted outside the United Services Club where a Union Jack flew at half mast and twenty tram men stood to attention. The interment took place at St Marylebone Cemetery and the Last Post was sounded. Maurice's wife Phyllis was left with two small children and she later remarried and had a son which she named Maurice after her late husband. Maurice junior subsequently went on to work as a mechanic at Edgware Garage and Phyllis later worked in the canteen at Muswell Hill bus garage, so the family was steeped in transport. There is a sad postscript to the story; in the last few years before the accident Edgar Kent, the conductor of the car, had more than his share of sorrow. In 1924 two young relatives perished in a fire that occurred at his house, and his wife died the following year. It later transpired that Thomas Colyer of Summers Lane, Finchley, the only other motorman to have driven *Bluebell*, should have been driving but it was his rest day. He went on to drive trams, and then buses, for forty-seven years until he retired at seventy.

After the crash, with a new roof and repainted into MET's standard red livery. The MSC plate on the front door shows the No.1963. (© TfL from the London Transport Museum Collection)

Experimental car No.330 in Ballards Lane. The modernity of the new tram contrasts with the rest of the traffic. (Commercial postcard)

Whilst *Bluebell* was being repaired the decision was taken to install a new domed roof in place of the flat one it had originally carried and the doors were widened. It returned to service early in 1928 but only operated between Whetstone and Cricklewood. In 1931 it was repainted red and when the LPTB took over METs activities in July 1933 it was renumbered 2255. Five years later it was scrapped.

With the experience gained with *Bluebell*, the UERL set about designing a car that would match the bus for speed and comfort. It would also be able to take advantage of a new higher speed limit of 20mph that had been introduced in 1926. Three experimental cars were produced by the Union Construction & Finance Company of Feltham. The new trams were to become known as Felthams and they certainly set new standards. Two of the prototypes, cars numbers 320 and 330, were built in 1929 and operated on route 40 (Whetstone–Cricklewood). At 40ft 11½ins long they were 5ft longer than *Bluebell* and were intended to incorporate the best features of motor cars, buses and Underground trains. The bodies tapered so they were wider at the waist (7ft 1¾in) than at the roof (6ft 8in) and they had seating for sixty-four passengers (twenty-two of them in the lower saloon) plus ten standing in each of the two vestibules. There were two sets of folding doors on each side; the ones at the rear, which were the entrance doors, were twice the width of the ones at the front, which were for exiting only. Both the upper and lower saloons had lateral, spring-upholstered seats; the ones in the lower saloon were in grey moquette and the ones in the upper saloon were covered with a grained red rexine. The driving cabs stood proud of the main body and for the first time the motorman could sit down at his job on a seat attached to the rear door of his cab.

No.330 was designed to test out the idea of passengers paying as they boarded and the conductor sat at a ticket machine just inside the entrance doors. To make sure that passengers did not avoid payment, the staircases were reversed, so that it was not possible to go upstairs without first passing the conductor. The system might have worked if there had been a flat fare for all journeys, but the large number of different tickets that had to be issued meant that congestion at the entrances caused boarding problems and conventional roving conductors were reinstated.

A third prototype, No.331, and nicknamed *Cissie*, was built in 1930 and differed from the other two in that it had one pair of air-operated doors in the centre of each side. The theory behind this layout was that it would be easier for the conductor to supervise the boarding and alighting of passengers, however it not only caused congestion, but also reduced the amount of standing room available. The experiment was not a success and eventually two conductors had to be employed, one on each deck.

Feltham car No.360 is about to turn left from the High Road into Woodhouse Road on its way to Holborn on service 21. This view is undated but it must have been before 1935 because Kingsway has not yet been built. (Commercial postcard)

With the experience gained from the experimental cars it was decided to build 100 new cars, fifty-four of which would go to the MET and forty-six to the LUT. The production Felthams, which cost £3,503 each, entered service on Wednesday 1 February 1931 on route 40 (Whetstone–Cricklewood). They were to introduce levels of comfort and speed never before experienced on London tramcars. They were not only quieter but they did not suffer from the rolling and pitching that the twenty-five-year-old trams were prone to. The sheer size of the Felthams meant that they could not operate on route 19 to Barnet because at the foot of Barnet Hill, under the railway bridge, the tracks were too close together to allow for such long vehicles to pass each other. Their size also meant that Finchley depot had to be enlarged by some 50ft at the eastern end and considerable structural changes had to be made, including the provision of an electrically powered traverser which ran on its own rails and allowed the cars to be moved sideways from one track in the depot to another. The modernity of the Felthams was emphasised by the continued use by the MET of open-topped trams; although some trams had been fitted with roofs, the programme was not completed until 1930. In contrast, all the LCC cars jointly operating the MET routes had covered top decks.

Improvements to the road layout at Tally Ho Corner were made in 1935 which made significant differences to the operation of the trams. Prior to this date both Ballards Lane on the western side and the High Road on the east carried two-way traffic of all kinds. Trams on routes 19, 40 and 60 would proceed north beyond this point to Whetstone or Barnet, whilst those on route 9 would terminate and reverse in Ballards Lane and those on route 21 would terminate and reverse in the High Road, outside Woolworths. The alterations involved building a new road, Kingsway, which linked Woodhouse Road to Ballards Lane, and the construction of a tram station alongside Nether Street, in effect creating a giant triangular roundabout. All vehicles had to travel north up Ballards Lane and south down the High Road, with trams terminating in the tram station having travelled clockwise round the system. The tram station included an office for the regulator and inspectors plus a modern concrete covered waiting area, in the style then being introduced by the LPTB and evident in many of their Underground and bus stations, such as Arnos Grove and Turnpike Lane.

The new trams introduced much greater standards of comfort. The upper deck of *Cissie* was light and airy and the leather seats on the upper deck were upholstered in bright blue. (Author)

The difference between the older type of tram and the new Felthams is graphically illustrated here. As well as advantages for passengers, at last the motorman could do his job without being exposed to the elements. MET 'H'-type tram No.271 and two Felthams are seen in Caledonian Road. The 'tombstone'-type of tram stop would be replaced by the familiar bullseye when LPTB took over in 1933. (M.J. O'Connor)

The new system inevitably produced its criticisms from motorists and residents. There was initially inadequate signposting, so that traffic coming from the north and wishing to go down Ballards Lane continued to try and do so, even though it was now a No Entry at this point. Eventually new 'Keep to the Left' signs were installed and drivers got used to turning right into Kingsway and then north or south into Ballards Lane. Many businesses complained bitterly about their loss of business; the Tally Ho pub claimed that they had lost so many customers that they might have to reduce their staff by three or four whilst the Belgrave Tavern, at the corner of Stanhope Road where the twenty-one trams used to terminate, bemoaned the fact that workmen were being forced to continue their journey to the tram station and they would not bother to retrace their steps to the Belgrave. Not surprisingly, The Cricketers pub next to the tram station in Nether Street welcomed the changes and thought they would be a great benefit to trade. Jelks, the furniture depository, reported a decrease of 25 per cent in trade but thought it would pick up in time while W.C. Davies, the tobacconists and confectioners at 736 High Road, said they were going to apply for rating re-assessment as they had lost so many tobacco buyers from the 9 and 21 trams. Woolworths reported that had seen no falling-off in trade but someone from Lilley & Skinner commented that, although they had not lost any customers, they had noticed the empty appearance of Tally Ho Corner which was formerly crowded with people, especially at night.

CHAPTER 7
TRAM MEN & WOMEN

In 1980 local historian Percy Reboul interviewed an ex-tram man, then in his seventies. His reminiscences give us an insight into the life and conditions of these dedicated public servants.

Tom Relf was born in 1908 in Wood Green and shortly afterwards his father died at the age of thirty-five. Tom's mother had also lost two little daughters and, to cap it all, Tom then lost another sister to tuberculosis at the age of twenty-three. Fortunately she had just had a little girl, Tom's niece, who later married one of Tom's cousins.

Tom's mother ran a successful boot shop at 214 Lordship Lane, Wood Green, employing three men. The shop also acted as a collection office for a laundry but, when the First World War came, the business had to close as the men were called up one by one, the last one being taken in June 1918.

The family moved up to Finchley to live with a cousin in 152 Woodhouse Road. The cousin's husband had been employed on the trams so the seeds were sown for Tom's later career. After leaving Finchley Central School at the age of fifteen, Tom had a number of jobs but decided, in 1930, to join MET, a job which had been recommended by the cousin. In those days jobs on the trams were not advertised, as seasonal staff were only taken to cover for the period May to September, when the regulars were taking their holidays.

Tom applied to METs office in Manor House and he arrived there for his interview at 9a.m. He was stuck in a room with the other applicants and they were left there until about 3p.m., when the interviewer merely said 'I'll let you know'. Tom was eventually taken on and began his training at Acton Broadway, which was a depot for the London United Tramways (LUT), a sister company for the MET and also for the South Metropolitan Electric Tramways (SMET).

Tom started training as a conductor, and a temporary one at that; this enabled him to learn the routes. They were taught about ticketing, which involved making sure that tickets issued tallied with the waybill which Tom described as a 'whacking bit of paper about 3ft by 2ft, with all the tickets in Christendom' listed down the side. The fare structure was so complicated that the tin box that he carried contained two, sometimes three, racks of Bell Punch tickets and dozens and dozens of different priced tickets. At the end of a shift the number of tickets issued and the money taken had to tally with the waybill, otherwise he had to make up the difference out of his own pocket. It usually took a quarter of an hour to cash up, and all calculations had to be done in the head – there were no calculators or ready reckoners. Needless to say, everyone in those days was taught mental arithmetic at school so this posed little problem. Tom described the job as exacting and accurate, but not difficult.

After a couple of years Tom was sent over to Acton again to train as a motorman (they were never called drivers) and he learnt initially on the mock-up of a tram. One of the features of the trams was the cowcatcher at the front, although it should really have been called a dog catcher. Horizontal wooden slats under the front would stop a stray dog from running under the tram and behind this was a wooden tray, also made up of slats, on which the dog would be deposited, frightened but unharmed.

Trainee motormen also had to be familiar with the mechanics of the tram and instructors would take a controller to pieces and the men would have to reassemble it. They would also be sent out of the room and deliberate faults would be created, which the men had to find on their return. Once, when they realised that no current was reaching the motor, they had to trace the fault back, and there was a piece of paper that had been carefully put between the wheel on the trolley head and the overhead wire. The training lasted about a fortnight and included driving a tram in service, with the motorman standing alongside to make sure things were done correctly. One old motorman gave Tom a tip: 'If you ever have a smash, don't upset yourself; just take a deep breath and hold it for some time!'

When Tom became a motorman, he became known as Mm. Relf and he worked almost exclusively on the 19 (Barnet to Tottenham Court Road) and 21 (North Finchley to Holborn) and was based at Finchley depot. Tom was living at Whetstone by then and used to cycle to the depot. One day, on the way to work, he parked his bike in the kerb and went into a shop to get some sandwiches; on the way out, a passing tram stopped and the motorman offered him a lift to the depot. After his duty was over he went to the shed to pick up his bike as usual only to realise what he had done; needless to say, when he got back to the shop the bike was gone. 'It must have been sold up the Caledonian Market by now,' said the police when he went to report its loss.

There were all kinds of rules and regulations and MET were very strict about their adherence. Conductors were supposed to collect all the fares in between fare stages because the conductor was supposed to be on the platform when the next stage was reached. Woe betide any conductor who was caught by a jumper (ticket inspector) with uncollected fares from the last stage or, worse still, the stage before that. A man from Head Office would be down to tick him off and it would go onto his record. If the record was too bad he would be dismissed or, if he was a seasonal man, he wouldn't be invited back the next May. The worst thing a motorman could do was to run early; this was severely frowned upon as it disrupted the schedule and would lead to gaps appearing.

Another thing the jumpers were on the look out for was 'punching on the line'. The Bell Punch tickets had the numbers of the fare stages listed on them, with lines between each one. Conductors were required to punch the ticket so that the hole appeared in the last fare stage for the fare paid. This made it easy for the jumper to see if people were overriding; however, on a crowded, swaying car it was easy to get the punch in the wrong place. Jumpers were a suspicious breed and would assume that the conductor had done it deliberately, whereas the conductor would swear blind that the tram had lurched just as he was punching the ticket. These tickets were known as 'deaf and dumb' tickets as the fare stages only had numbers, not names.

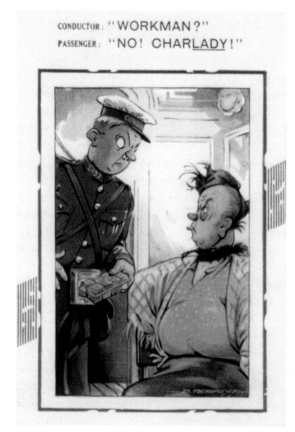

Below: In Finchley depot the inside of car No.317 is about to be vacuum cleaned, utilising the overhead system that was installed in 1928, enabling a car to be cleaned and overhauled in less than six minutes. At a demonstration to the local press in 1931 the MET's general manager demonstrated the pulling power of the vacuum cleaners and lost a penny in the process. He declined to repeat the experiment using a shilling! (© TfL from the London Transport Museum Collection)

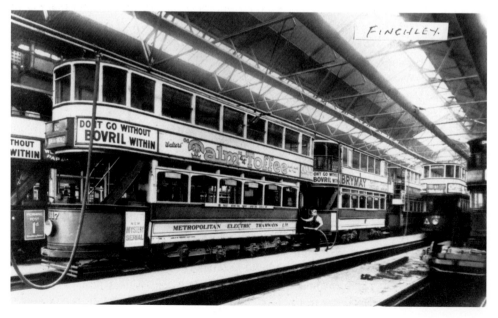

Generally, relations between motormen and their conductors were good, however a bad driver could give a rough ride, which was bad for the passengers as well as his conductor and, if he drove too fast, the conductor would have less time to collect all the fares (sometimes as many as twenty or thirty people would get on at a stop) before the next fare stage.

Motormen had to drive to try and adhere to the timetable, and they would try and break the journey up into 5-minute segments. For example, the running time between Barnet and Finchley (two and a half miles) was 15 minutes, with a fare stage at Station Road Barnet (No.27), another at Whetstone (No.25) and then North Finchley (No.23). Although the distance between Barnet and Station Road was only half a mile, it was on a steep incline so 5 minutes would be allowed as the tram had to descend using the magnetic brake; for the remaining two segments, which were on the flat, 5 minutes each could easily be allowed. On one hot, sleepy Sunday afternoon there were few people about so Tom wasn't really paying attention. He then found himself in trouble at Highgate with a jumper known as 'Razor' Sharp. Tom had arrived at The Woodman, Highgate when he should only have been at The Wellington so he was running about 3 minutes early. 'Whatever are you doing, Relf? I don't know what you're about.' Tom said that Sharp was as genuinely upset as if he had pinched his gold watch. 'This really is too bad!' was Sharp's parting shot.

The first tram went out from the depot at about 4a.m. and, because Tom loved his sleep, he would invariably offer to swap his early shifts with other men so that he could have a lie-in. This made him popular because the early shift was noticeably easier. On one 6a.m. shift Tom's conductor was absent and a replacement conductor, a lady, was waiting for him. Tom said 'Are you with me today?' and she replied 'Yes. It's my first day.' When he asked her what time she got up she said '*Four o'clock!*' It turned out that she lived in Barnet and had walked all the way.

Motormen had to be a hardy breed as the early trams had no windscreens, these did not come along until 1929 and even then the older trams were not converted. In the winter Tom wore thick woollen underwear, Melton trousers, a three-quarter-length pea jacket, an overcoat and an oilskin and he still felt as though he was wearing nothing at all. In summer they would wear white dustcoats with white covers on their hats. Although they weren't issued, Tom always wore gauntlets. At first they were allowed to keep the old uniforms when new ones were issued, but when the Second World War came along the old uniforms had to be handed in. This was unpopular with the men, particularly as many of them had allotments and they were, in Tom's words, 'too bloody poor to have a suit. They used to be walking around in tram uniforms most of the time.'

Tom recalled that around 1930 the pay was £3 12s 0d a week, or 12s a day, about the same as the police. By comparison, a labourer would be getting around £2 10s 0d. On Sundays they were supposed to get a quarter of an hour's overtime, but they were required to work four journeys (for 16s) instead of the normal three journeys (for 12s). Tom recalls his wife asking if he had had good week: 'Yes, £4, and many the time my wife would walk out with a sixpence in her pocket and I would only have sixpence in my pocket. A cup of tea in the canteen was a penny so my big spending was a cup of tea every day!'

Holidays were very strange. You did not get a holiday until you had been there three years, and then you got ten days. Tom said the holidays seemed to be drawn out of a hat, and the people doing the drawing seemed to be union officials, who invariably got June and July! For several years Tom got September but he seemed to recall that the weather at the time was very

MET motormen and conductors pose outside the shelter at the Craven Park terminus.
(Andrew Forsyth Collection)

nice. In 1933 the holiday period was extended from the traditional May to September to all the
year round. Tom said this meant he was sometimes given a holiday in December or January!
Despite all the hardships, Tom enjoyed his work and claimed that tram men took a pride in
giving their passengers a good ride.

Another tram man, conductor Frederick Harvey, was also interviewed by Percy Reboul and he
recalled that if a passenger had passed a dud coin on to the conductor and he then tried to pay it
in at the end of his shift, the clerk would break the coin in half and the conductor would have to
make up the shortfall from his own pocket. Conductors who were rude to passengers would be
suspended for a day without pay or, in extreme cases, would be dismissed. Fred recalled that he
used to fill up his white billy can with tea from a restaurant near the Swan & Pyramids. The tea
would cost twopence and a beef dripping doorstep sandwich cost a penny and it would be eaten, a
bit at a time, in quiet periods between collecting fares.

He had no break at midday and no proper meal until he got home in the evening. Later on, the
union managed to negotiate a 20-minute break but by the time Fred had walked from Tally Ho to
Finchley depot it was time to go back. On a typical shift Fred would start at 4a.m. from Finchley
depot, go to Barnet and then work 8½ hours straight off without a break, during which time he
would do four journeys from Barnet to Tottenham Court Road. He used to work seven days
straight off and when he did get a day off he would go in at 1.30p.m. on a Sunday and by the time
he had finished his roster, paid in his takings and walked home it was almost time to start work
again, so in fact it was not a rest day, just half a day. They had seven days holiday, but it did not start
until Sunday, so his wife and children would go off on the Saturday and he would join them on the
following day. On one occasion an inspector instructed Fred to give a lady a ticket, even though
she had no money. Fred had to make up the money from his own pocket and about a month later
he was called in to the office and given three one-penny stamps in payment!

Another local resident, Hilda Clark, who was a schoolgirl at Queen Elizabeth's Grammar School between 1934 and 1939, recalled the time when a conductor came to her rescue. She ran to catch the tram and as she jumped on the platform her case burst and all her books fell out. The kindly conductor kept the tram waiting while she picked everything up. Hilda lived in New Southgate and travelled to Barnet on a Feltham on the 21 to Tally Ho where she then changed to an E1-type tram on route 19 to Barnet. The journey took about an hour and the trams were full of schoolchildren from Woodhouse School, Christ's College Finchley and the Finchley Catholic Grammar School as well as her own. On Fridays it was cadet training day for the boys of Christ's College and Hilda recalls that the boys made a terrific row on the stairs of the trams with their boots.

Tram crews had very little time to take refreshment breaks and one lady who lived at number 16 Station Road, New Southgate, had a sideline that involved preparing tram men's teas. As the tram stopped outside her house the conductor would dash up to the front door and have his enamel tea can filled up from a big ornate brass urn that was kept on the table specially for the purpose.

Sometimes the roles would be reversed and passengers would help out tram crews. Late in the evening of Christmas Day 1937 rain had turned to sleet and sleet had turned to snow which fell the whole night and well into the morning of Boxing Day. A single-track service was operated along the Great North Road until 10.30a.m. on Boxing Day, after which the rails were cleared and a more or less normal service resumed, although this was occasionally interrupted when snow built up around the safety gates in the front of the trams. At this point drivers and conductors, and some of the passengers, dismounted and cleared the snow, using route boards that had been removed from the sides of the trams.

The General Strike of 1926 lasted nine days, from Tuesday 4 May to Wednesday 12 May and involved workers from all trades, including transport workers. At a meeting on the eve of the strike, at the Moss Hall Tavern, MET men voted unanimously to 'support the miners in their rightful demands'. The following day about a hundred men picketed Finchley depot and no trams ran. A union official said, 'You may take it from me there will be no trouble' and, although the police were in attendance, they were not required. No General buses ran, but the independents on routes 284 and 526 provided a service. An inspector said, 'If the public don't support the pirates now, they deserve no buses,' and they did, in fact, do a brisk trade for a couple of days, charging normal fares; a reporter on an Overground bus from East Finchley to Highgate claimed he was squashed by sixteen standing passengers. At East Finchley Station the only person there was the station master, accompanied by his dog.

By Saturday 8 May a tram service of sorts was being run by young student volunteers who acted as drivers and conductors; each tram had a Special Constable on board to prevent trouble. In the second week of the strike a number of people on bicycles attempted to hold up a No.40 tram near the North Circular Road. One of them, a sixteen-year-old lad wearing a red badge and with the front of his bicycle painted red jeered at the tram driver and called out: 'Two-a-penny tram drivers!' He was arrested and charged and was subsequently bound over and ordered to pay costs. There were a number of cases of stones, and even bricks, being hurled at trams and buses and several people were arrested but they were dealt with leniently by the courts. Normal services resumed on Thursday 13 May when the strike was called off.

Beatrice Dobie recalled some memories of her late grandfather, Joshua Kidd Bruce, who was influential in the running of LCC Tramways. He was born on 3 November 1871 at Westhill of Airlie in Angus/Forfarshire. He was the second child of Andrew Bruce and Catherine Anderson Kidd and was one of eight: five boys and three girls, one of whom, Emily, died in infancy. The family moved in his early childhood to Wester Jordanstone in Meigle, Perthshire where he attended Alyth School and he subsequently gained entry to the Veterinary School of Glasgow University at the age of fifteen. He qualified at nineteen and, as he could not practice until he was twenty-one, he spent the two years as a demonstrator in the Veterinary School, followed by a brief spell as a vet in either Ayr or Oban.

Bruce came south in about 1894 as Veterinary Officer of the London Tramways Company, where he was also responsible for the management of depots and stables, and pioneered the treatment of equine pneumonia. He made regular trips to Dublin and Brittany to buy horses for the trams and was asked to supply horses to the Royal Household, which gave him and his family a permanent pass to the Royal Mews.

Equipped with his Bell Punch machine, leather pouch, whistle and fashionable moustache, an LCC tram conductor awaits his passengers. (Commercial postcard)

In June 1903 he was appointed Traffic Manager and was married on 15 July 1908 to Beatrice Mary, younger daughter of John Smallwood of Smallwood, Cheshire. They made their home at 90 Talbot Road, Highgate, where they were the first residents of the house. For the rest of his life, he would start his holidays on 15 July, spending a month in Strathmore and a month in Kent. In 1925 Bruce was promoted to General Manager but he had already made a number of innovations including the introduction of the ones All Day Ticket and the modernisation of the tramcars (known as 'Pullmanisation') and he appeared to be a caring manager. He introduced half day working on Christmas Day; men with young families had the morning off, and those without worked the morning shift. Bruce believed that if he wanted Christmas Day with his children, so did his men. He used to support the company's sports days and attended whenever he could; he often took his daughter, Catherine, with him. At weekends, he would sometimes take his children with him and follow a tram route from one end to the other to see how they were running and to show an interest in the men. One route he regularly used was the section from Archway to Barnet.

Although he sympathised with the strikers in their support of the miners, he felt he had a duty to keep London moving and he went on air to say that the men must either return to work or hand in their uniforms as they would be deemed to have resigned. During the General Strike his death was erroneously reported in the Government's emergency newspaper and he rang his wife to reassure her that he was not dead. She assured him that she did not believe he was speaking to her from the other side! On one occasion Bruce personally visited a conductress who had broken her leg and he was distressed to learn that she had put her leg out to try and stop her tram slipping back down a hill; she believed the management would be upset if it got damaged.

The Bruce family had a bulldog who once rode on the platform of a tram. Passengers were somewhat dubious boarding around him and the conductor was equally reluctant to approach what was, apparently, a gentle, kind dog. Bruce's wife was summoned and she boarded another tram to fetch the dog. Beatrice Dobie always thought that he had only made one such journey, but she later learned that he was a frequent traveller!

Although Bruce had come south to look after horses, he managed the transition to electricity happily, however he believed that the introduction of trolleybuses was a retrograde step as he thought that the overhead wires would be dangerous in the event of aerial war; the LCC, of course, mainly used conduit throughout their system.

Beatrice recalls that her mother, Catherine, was asked to suggest a new colour for the trams' livery. She chose claret and it looked appalling; she was delighted when it was repainted in due course.

CHAPTER 8
EVERYDAY OCCURRENCES

Urban myths about trams usually concern stories of cyclists getting their wheels caught in the tramlines and ending up at the depot. In practice tramlines could be dangerous, particularly in wet weather, as one sad story illustrates. At 11a.m. on Thursday 14 April 1927 a twelve-year-old boy, Dennis George Loveless of Friern Watch Avenue, was cycling northwards along East Finchley High Road with his brother. He overtook a six-wheel steam wagon with a trailer and, after cutting in front of it, his bicycle skidded on the tram line and he fell off a few feet in front of the lorry. The driver tried to brake but could not stop in time and the boy was run over and killed instantly. The back wheel of his bicycle was buckled and the hub was driven deep into the wood block paving. Unfortunately it took over an hour to find a doctor and the boy lay in the road covered with a sack and a policeman's cape. Tram services were held up for a while but the service resumed when northbound cars were switched to the opposite track. Had the boy lived he would have celebrated his thirteenth birthday on the following Saturday.

In January the previous year a less serious accident occurred, although the cause was the same. A Jowett two-seater car was proceeding along Ballards Lane when it turned to the centre of the road to avoid some repairs. The car skidded on the tram lines, struck the offside of an oncoming tram, turned two complete circles, mounted the pavement, rebounded from a wall and overturned. Not surprisingly, although the car was wrecked, damage to the tram was slight. Fortunately the only injury suffered by the driver was a cut to his hand. Danger was not confined to the track: in one incident in 1927 a trolley wheel fell off at North Finchley and penetrated the roof of a car. Tram lines served one useful purpose for motorists however. During the many fogs that London suffered from in those days, motorists could comfortably follow trams, at a distance of course, secure in the knowledge that they would not get lost, although they might end up in Finchley depot!

On Sunday 7 May 1922 two accidents occurred near the De Dion Works at 989 High Road, North Finchley, both involving trams. Road works had been taking place for many weeks and width was restricted to two lines of traffic. A motor car heading towards Barnet had stopped at the obstruction, only to be hit from behind by a tram and forcing it onto the pavement. 25 minutes later, while witnesses were still giving evidence to the police, another car was hit from behind by a tram, this one travelling at 15mph. Witnesses said the motorman was looking at the previous accident. The prosecuting counsel was particularly scathing:

I say again what I have said elsewhere, that the LCC tram drivers never give any assistance to the police. This tram driver not only refused to give evidence as to what had occurred, but was actually rude. The representatives of the LCC will not assist the police, and will not make a statement at all. They might have a good explanation, but they will not give it. What their explanation is in this case, I don't know.

Both motormen were fined 40s, the maximum, and costs and expenses were imposed.

In 1935 *Punch* carried a sarcastic piece on trams which probably accurately summed up the feelings of the time towards the viability of trams on roads increasingly occupied by cars:

'If,' begun Uncle Henry, who had just returned from the first trip in his new car – 'if I drove continuously at a fixed distance from the edge of the road and refused to pull in to the left to allow other people to pass me I should be accused of obstruction?'

'Undoubtedly,' I said. 'Or again,' he continued, 'if I wished to overtake someone ahead, instead of going out to the right, hooted until he moved out of the way, I should be looked upon as a public nuisance?'

'Very probably.'

'B'-type car No.22 picks up passengers outside the entrance to New Southgate Station. The central portion of the road, alongside the tram tracks, was maintained by the MET, but the poor condition of the surface on the margins was down to the local council. The station master's house is on the left. (Commercial postcard)

A foggy day in London town, but trams would always find their way home. (Commercial postcard)

'Furthermore, if I would not draw in to the kerb to allow a passenger to alight, but stopped without warning in the middle of the road and expected other traffic to wait until he had strolled across to the footpath, my conduct would not be tolerated?'

Again I agreed.

'And I take it that the fault would be aggravated if I drove without a number plate, had no proper headlights after dark and stamped continuously on a large gong?'

This time he did not wait for an answer, but went on at an increasing rate.

'And if my unspeakable behaviour were aggravated by defects in the deplorable vehicle with which I encumbered the road, I am sure that that would not extenuate the offence. And, if the so-called vehicle required a light railway track along the centre of the road on which to run, would I be allowed to lay it?'

'Certainly not,' I said.

'And yet,' he concluded with a triumphant gleam, 'the TRAMS do all these things and no one lifts a finger or says a word. Why?'

To put this diatribe into context, in 1935 there were 1.5 million cars on the road; ten years previously the figure had been only 692,800, so trams now had to contend with more than twice as much traffic.

In 1931 the Ministry of Transport issued a draft Highway Code which contained the following paragraph:

Subject to any local provisions to the contrary, tram cars may be overtaken on the near side, but in this case special caution is necessary. Watch carefully to see if passengers are boarding the tram car or alighting from it before you pass: in any case go slow.

Friern Barnet Council objected to this and suggested that it should be compulsory for all traffic to be prohibited from passing stationary trams on the near side. The Highways Committee of Barnet Council discussed the matter but declined to support Friern Barnet as they did not consider it would be possible to enforce this without a police presence.

Maintenance to that section of the roads occupied by tram tracks continued to be funded centrally, rather than by the local authorities. By early May 1925 the foundations of the wood-paved sections of Friern Barnet Road had become defective and had to be made good. The cost of £600 was paid for by the Middlesex County Council and Ministry of Transport, not by Friern Barnet UDC. In fact, around this time the Middlesex County Council were proposing to introduce a Bill which would enable the council to take over the repair of all tram tracks, clearly as a result of MET's failure to maintain them in good condition. One local resident recalled that the rails in Friern Barnet Road needed to be cleaned out periodically. His father, who was a child at the time, let fly with a catapult at the maintenance men bending over the rails. The child was a cross-country runner, so he escaped without getting caught!

CHAPTER 9

SCRAP THE TRAMS

It was during the mid-1920s that dissatisfaction with the tramways came to a head; even Lord Ashfield, Chairman of the UERL seemed unsure of their future. In a speech in March 1927 to the annual meeting of the London and Suburban Traction Company he announced that the receipts of the MET were short of the bare working expenses by £3,844 and that the company had notified the MCC that they could not entertain a renewal of their lease, which was due to expire in 1930, unless a drastic change were to be effected in the circumstances under which the tramways were operated.

The public were vocal in their criticisms and there were proposals for local authorities to take over the tramways from the Combine. There was even a movement to 'Scrap the Trams'. It is worth quoting at length from a letter to the *Finchley Press* in 1927 which highlighted some of the grievances felt by critics.

A Mr J. Foxley Norris, obviously a motorist, wrote:

I maintain that the time has come to take up the tram lines and scrap the cars. For 50 years I have suffered from the dangers of tram lines: every cyclist will tell you that it is usual for him yearly to have two or three skids on the lines. I have seen a light car try to turn on to the lines to avoid a stationary car, but the line would not allow it, and the driver was positively thrown off the lines and butted into a stationary car. My worst two accidents were caused by the trams, because now that motor cars are increasing, the trams congest the space on the road and the motor driver has to choose between running down tram passengers, or going on his wrong side to butt into a motor car that cannot avoid him.

We are asked to express an opinion as to the new luxurious cars. My answer is short: 'Unnecessary Extravagance.' As the trams do not now pay expenses, the LCC think that, by spending more ratepayers' money to give a luxurious car they will entice passengers to travel by them. Weakmindness: for do the LCC or any sensible thinkers think it will stem the ultimate scrapping of the trams? The passengers do not require more comfortable carriages, but they require more convenience, safer travelling and less expense. They prefer to be landed at the kerb, instead of fixed points in the middle of the road, to avoid the risk of being run into. The pace of the cars was increased, but the motor 'bus can go faster. The 'bus can, if the road is congested, take a side street, and alter the route to suit the travellers. It is not fair trading because your business does not pay to stop your adversary doing his best; and although I have lost money in motor bus companies I still am fair enough to see justice done to them.

If the trams were removed, the roads would be cleaner and less congested for all other users.

The motor 'bus companies would supply enough carriages to take the place of the tramcars at once. If the LCC hesitate, because of their staff, then I suggest they build motor 'buses, put the conductors and drivers on them, and other workers in similar employment – pension off, as they must eventually, the veterans and form the remaining officers into directors and shareholders of the motor 'bus companies, giving them shares in proportion to their retiring allowances. It will rest with them whether they make fortunes, or lose them, without troubling the ratepayers to make up the loss.

Interestingly, two weeks after that letter was published, the paper reported that a 'Commission of German Engineers and Traffic Experts' had visited London with a view to coming up with ideas to solving Berlin's traffic problem. Their recommendation was that trams were a better solution than buses because of their ability to carry large numbers of passengers, thus reducing the number of vehicles required, and leading to less traffic congestion. In defence of the trams, one correspondent wrote:

The trams of Finchley have been one of the prime factors in its development. They provide a service of cars at all hours of the day, besides providing healthy recreation for masses of City workers. The issue of workmen's tickets affords regular employment to a considerable number of local residents, besides running cars at some periods at a complete loss, at the public requirements. The number of accidents caused by trams is surprisingly small in comparison with other vehicles and undoubtedly a good many of these accidents would be prevented if all motor drivers were forced to keep to a 12mph speed limit. All drivers should be subject to a test, before being allowed on the streets. The convictions at the Local Police Court proves the utter disregard for law and order, of a good many motorists passing through Finchley. Abolish the Tram-car, the position of Finchley would be deplorable. The 'buses would be no substitute, they would require three 'buses per minute to cope with rush hour traffic, and as they would only be required about four hours each day, the results would not be economical.

At a meeting of the Church End Ratepayers Association in May 1927 Councillor Pinching put the case for the trams. They were not only essential in keeping competing traffic facilities up to the mark, he said, but they also provided facilities in the early mornings and late evenings and they also saved the ratepayers immense sums in street widening and road maintenance.

Tram fares were a source of dissatisfaction as well. In February 1922 the Finchley Ratepayers' Defence League wrote to the MET complaining that although the LCC had reduced their 1.5*d* fares to 1*d*, the MET had not followed suit. The reply from the General Manger of MET was not very encouraging:

My Company will be very glad to adopt any system of fares which would tend to increase revenue. They do not think, however, that the rate of charge adopted by the LCC would have that effect. Your League will, of course, appreciate the essential difference of municipal undertakings, such as the London County Council, who are providing the necessary revenue to meet the tramway expenditure partly from passengers and partly from ratepayers, and a company which has to depend entirely on passengers for revenue. If the LCC successfully demonstrate that by reducing their fares they at least maintain their revenue, my company will not hesitate to follow.

Needless to say, the MET never did reduce their fares; indeed, their financial position made this impossible. The success of the Independents in running buses in competition to the trams from 1922 onwards was, of course, one of the contributory factors to the decline in the MET's revenue and in December 1926 the Independent Omnibus Proprietors of London mischievously entered the fray by writing to the MCC and suggesting that MET's lease should not be renewed after 1930; not surprisingly, they offered to operate buses in place of trams. In August 1927 the MCC decided that they were unable to take over running of the trams from the MET, despite the latter being in arrears on payments to the tune of £123,000 and the fact that they had been in default to the council since December 1925.

Talk of scrapping the trams ignored the financial consequences of writing off over £2 million of investment in their infrastructure and the subsequent costs of dismantling the system, so their future was assured in the short term, although the seeds had been sown and their eventual demise was only four years away.

CHAPTER 10

A FOND FAREWELL

Although the Feltham trams had been superior in many respects to the new generation of motor buses, as we have seen the days of the trams were numbered. As well as holding up other traffic, the act of boarding or alighting from a tram in the centre of the road had become increasingly hazardous for passengers, and the expansion of the Underground network and the electrification of suburban rail lines offered attractive alternatives to commuters. The LPTB came into being on 1 July 1933 and was immediately responsible for running all buses, trams and tubes in London. Almost one of their first decisions was to replace the inflexible tram with the more flexible trolleybus.

The first trolleybuses in London had actually been introduced in May 1931 by the LUT in the Teddington, Kingston and Dittons area and they proved to be a great success. Not only were the four-wheel 'Diddlers' (the nickname for the new trolleybuses) speedy, quiet and comfortable but they were proving to be cheaper to run than trams and they were attracting more passengers. It is somewhat ironic that it was the LUT that had been responsible for the development of the Felthams, the last word in tram modernity, which came into service in the same year.

In May 1934 the LPTB had a Bill passed by Parliament authorising the conversion of ninety miles of the tramway network to trolleybuses, although routes in the Finchley area were not amongst them. Gradually new Bills were introduced in Parliament and former tram routes gave way to trolleybuses. It is worth noting that the LPTB really only ever saw trolleybuses as a straight replacement for trams; there was virtually no expansion of the network.

The last tram to leave Barnet did so at midnight on Saturday 5 March 1938, having left Tally Ho at 11.45p.m., 5 minutes behind schedule. LPTB officials had stated that there would be no ceremonial to mark the occasion, but nevertheless car No.2238 was draped with two Union Jacks, one at either end. The driver was Mr A. Lowe of 34 Kingsmeade, Barnet, and the conductor Mr F. Mardell, of 34 Lambert Road, North Finchley, who had worked on the first ever tram to Barnet; in fact Mr Mardell had worked on the route continuously since it started. On board was the man who, thirty-one years earlier had been the first passenger. Mr Herbert J. Bee of New Barnet had, with a friend, boarded a tram at Junction Road on Thursday 28 March 1907 for a journey to his work in High Street, Barnet, a journey he had previously been doing by train from Holloway where he then lived. They were unaware that they were helping to inaugurate the new system until they looked at their tickets, which were numbered A0000 and A0001.

Whilst the send-off at Tally Ho was somewhat subdued, the scene at the Barnet terminus was altogether different. A crowd of 400 or 500 had gathered on either side of the road and on the newly erected traffic island, where the war memorial once stood. Many of the crowd were in

The Last Car
from Barnet

(Commercial postcard)

evening dress and photographers and newsreel men were there to record the scene; cars were hooting and police were holding back people who were trying to board the vehicle. Most of the light bulbs, and anything moveable, had been taken for souvenirs, messages were chalked on the woodwork and the windows and the car started on its journey down Barnet Hill, followed by a procession of motor cars all honking their horns and with their headlights on.

Although some passengers had left at Station Road, New Barnet and Totteridge Lane, most stayed on until the tram reached the Grand Hall Cinema at 690-700 High Road, North Finchley, where more people forced their way on. When it reached Tally Ho it did two laps round the Gaumont Cinema and when it finally stopped it was surrounded by crowds of people who proceeded to take the Union Jacks, the indicator boards, handles and even nuts and bolts and screws. Someone tried to cut the rope holding the trolley arm but he was restrained by an inspector. An LPTB official said, 'While trophies taken from the tram are officially stolen property, the trophy hunters need not fear the Board may take proceedings against them.' Two policemen intervened, some semblance of order was restored and No.2238 went into Finchley depot where new bulbs were fitted for the last lap of its journey to Wood Green Depot. Mr Bee said: 'I never expected such a fuss as this. I'm glad it's been like this and it has been a swell farewell to the good old trams. I shall feel kind of lost without them, though.' Mr Mardell reported that he had sold 200 tickets from North Finchley to Barnet and back on the night.

The journey to Wood Green depot was equally eventful as the *Barnet Press* reported:

Tram
to
Trolleybus

On and from Sunday, 2nd Aug., Trolleybuses will be substituted for Trams on the routes below:

TRAM		TROLLEYBUS	
ROUTE	BETWEEN	ROUTE	BETWEEN
45	Whetstone and Cricklewood	645	North Finchley (Tally Ho Corner) and Edgware (Station Road) via Cricklewood Broadway
60	N. Finchley and Paddington	660	North Finchley (Tally Ho Corner) and Hammersmith Broadway via Cricklewood, Craven Park and Acton (High Street)

Tram routes 62 and (at weekday peak-hours) 64 from Paddington will connect with Trolleybuses at Craven Park. Workman transfer facilities will be provided between Tally Ho Corner and Paddington. At weekday peak-hours Tram route 9 will be extended from Tally Ho Corner to Whetstone (Totteridge Lane).

LONDON TRANSPORT

LC.614

TRAM TO TROLLEYBUS

On Sunday next, 6th March, Trolleybuses will be substituted for Trams on the existing routes 9, 17 and 21

BARNET and MOORGATE.
(CHURCH)   (FINSBURY SQUARE)
609 daily via Highgate, Holloway Road and the Angel.

BARNET and GOLDERS GREEN
(CHURCH)   (UNDERGROUND)
651 daily via Church End, Finchley. Route extended outside the peak hours to Cricklewood (Walm Lane).

N. FINCHLEY and HOLBORN
(TALLY HO)   (CIRCUS)

VIA HIGHGATE & KINGS CROSS		VIA WOOD GN. & KINGS CROSS	
517	617	521	621
WEEKDAYS	DAILY	DAILY	DAILY

Routes 517 and 521: to Holborn Circus via Grays Inn Rd.; returning via Charterhouse St. and Farringdon Rd. Routes 617 and 621: to Holborn Circus via Farringdon Rd. and Charterhouse St.; returning via Grays Inn Rd.

TRAMS The following routes will be withdrawn : 9, 13, 17, 19, 21, 39a, 51 ; the section of 71 between Wood Green (Underground) Station and Aldersgate. Route 39 will run daily between Bruce Grove and Wood Green (Underground) Station only ; route 41 will be extended from Manor House Station to Winchmore Hill.
BUSES Route 45 will run via Aldersgate to Holloway Road Garage in place of Tram route 13.

LN.115.38

The tram tracks come up in Bounds Green Road in September 1965. (Ron Kingdon)

While the tracks are being removed in the trolleybus station at North Finchley, temporary wires were erected in Old Nether Street, on the right, so that services were uninterrupted. (Ron Kingdon Collection)

Great doings in Friern Barnet on Saturday night as the last 21 tram rumbled down Woodhouse Road, along Friern Barnet Road and thence to the Wood Green depot, the happy hunting ground of trams whose work is done. Not by any stretch of the imagination can the passing of the tram service be described as mournful, for the large crowd assembled at Tally Ho Corner for the express purpose of speeding the last car on its way was in exceedingly high spirits. Cheers and whoops of joy greeted the lumbering red monster as it drew into the tram station, and within a few minutes the car was full with passengers standing upstairs, downstairs, and on the platforms. One clang of the bell, and the tram trundled into the Great North Road, clattered over the points and swaying, banging and crashing, was away on its last journey along Woodhouse Road. On board all was chaos, and although no serious damage was committed, the revellers thoroughly enjoyed their farewell party. Movable objects were appropriated as souvenirs; messages were chalked on the woodwork and the windows and as gestures of defiance, the seat cushions were removed and turned over. Thus did the last tram pass.

Mr Lowe and Mr Mardell got a lift in a motor car and followed No.2238 to Wood Green; on the way Mr Lowe said: 'Give me the old open trams for health. You had to face all weathers – cold biting winds, hail, snow, rain and hot blistering summer days – but, by golly it made you feel good, except when your moustache got frozen.' When he was asked if he had minded getting home in the early hours when he had worked late turns he replied: 'I rather enjoy it as a matter of fact. It keeps me fit. In fact I often have chances of lifts home, but I refuse, preferring to walk.' And so the trams faded into history, but the dedication of men like Mr Lowe and Mr Mardell meant that they would live in affection in people's memories for many years.

CHAPTER 11

A NEW BEGINNING

Under London Transport's tram replacement programme, the first tram routes in the area to be converted were the 40 and 60. These were replaced by trolleybus routes 645 and 660 on Sunday 2 August 1936 although the new routes were somewhat different. The 645 went from North Finchley but then beyond Cricklewood to Edgware and the 660 went as far as Craven Park but then continued on to Hammersmith instead of terminating at Paddington.

The changeover appeared to go smoothly although a couple of incidents were reported that seem to indicate that perhaps trolleybus drivers, who were in the main ex-tram motormen, were having difficulty getting used to their new steeds. The first reported accident came two days after their introduction, when a trolleybus on route 645 crashed into a traction pole at Granville Road and, although nobody was hurt, the front was extensively damaged. A more humorous incident was reported by the *Finchley Press* on 7 August:

> One driver, obviously having a trial run, was early presented with a road problem. These vehicles are comparatively silent running and on this occasion a small dog in the act of performing the pedestrians' most annoying habit – crossing the road diagonally – was strolling unconcernedly across the main thoroughfare. Warnings were unheeded and the driver, apparently forgetting after many years on the trams that he could direct his vehicle where he wished, pulled up. M'lord stopped, turned to his nearside and passed behind the bus. An excellent example of road sense.

In the same issue of the paper, in his 'Motoring Notes' column, Mr O. Brent Brook somewhat pompously welcomed the coming of the trolleybus with these words:

> Shopkeepers and residents along Ballards Lane and Regents Park Road hailed Sunday last as the day of deliverance from that obsolete form of transport – the tramcar. It does not fall within my province to tell you of the unanimous golden opinions of main road residents and users of public service vehicles, but I can tell you that with the passing of the tramcar from one of Finchley's main arteries there has disappeared from the motorists' vision a very noisy and cumbersome obstruction, which was the cause, directly or indirectly, of an appreciable number of accidents. Here's hoping that the Great North Road may speedily be freed from the juggernauts which always hug the crown of the road, and which, perforce, discharge their human cargo in the middle of the highway between two lines of traffic. Such a state of affairs will surely be a universal memory of the past within a few years. However, we motorists must

be fair and kindly for a while and remember that most of the trolleybus drivers have never previously steered any vehicle. Hugging the tramlines will be a natural tendency for some little time, but it does one's eyesight good to see the new gliders float in towards the kerb to pick up and set down.

A week later the sentiments about trams were echoed by a correspondent who wrote:

Often have complaints been made about traffic conditions in Ballards Lane, Finchley. The latest improvement by way of the trolleybuses is such that on all sides one hears nothing but praise. The bus is roomy, light and yet plain and simple in construction, and gives passengers a feeling of heaven at last. But, above all, the elimination of the row and rattle of the trams is the greatest blessing, and for such the responsible powers deserve the greatest thanks.

An early criticism of boarding arrangements at Golders Green Station was made by a correspondent who requested that during evening rush hours Tube passengers should be allowed to board trolleybuses at the new roundabout rather than having to cross the main road. Within a few weeks theses changes were made, to the benefit of both passengers and other traffic.

Bright and early on the hot sunny morning of Sunday 6 March 1938, the first trolleybuses on routes 617, 521, 621 and 609, described in the local press as 'gleaming red juggernauts', glided smoothly into service. The following day, Monday 7 March, routes 517:

New trolleybuses at Hendon depot stand alongside the trams they would soon replace. (D.W.K. Jones)

An E1 tram, No.318, and a Feltham share the space with the new trolleybuses at North Finchley Station. The trams are using the positive wire on the new trolleybus overhead. (D.W.K. Jones)

Just opposite the Gaumont Cinema in High Road, North Finchley, a tower wagon is in attendance, presumably to effect some repairs to the overhead. Trolleybus No.90, with route blind reading 'Special', is on driver training duties. (D.W.K. Jones)

shepherded their charges carefully among the traffic, and driving with a dignity that was becoming of one in whose care was such a fine vehicle as a new LPTB trolleybus. The latter evidenced their pride in their treatment of the passengers. The ticket punch seemed to jingle more merrily, change was always forthcoming without the usual gruff 'Haven't you got anything smaller?' and a gracious smile was the reward of passengers who commented on the excellence of the new buses.

The most overworked phrase in Friern Barnet was: 'What do you think of the new trolleybuses?' Just as on the first day of tram operation, the public of Barnet turned out in their hundreds and people were taking one penny rides down Barnet Hill and back again just to say they had ridden on a trolleybus. The public were advised that the substitution of trolleybuses for trams would make the street much quieter, especially at intersections where tram rails had crossed, but they were also warned that the quietness of trolleybuses would surprise people who were not accustomed to them and pedestrians were advised to exercise special care when stepping off the pavement. Parents and teachers were asked to explain to children the characteristics of the new vehicles.

Although the service was promised to be at the same level as the trams, initially it seems to have left a lot to be desired, particularly in terms of frequency. A Major S. Crowley, writing to the *Barnet Press* on 1 April 1938, referred to the 'banana service' because when the buses did eventually come, they did so in bunches. The 521 and 621 seemed to be less frequent than the 609; the Major reports waiting at Tally Ho and seeing eighteen buses heading for Golders Green and only one going to Wood Green. Another correspondent reported waiting 23 minutes at the Horsham Avenue stop at 9a.m. for a bus to Bounds Green and then, at 6.25p.m. the same evening, waiting 24 minutes at Bounds Green Station for a bus going to Finchley. When a belated procession arrived, they were already full and there was only room for two or three passengers at a time.

Eventually things settled down and timings, together with the greater speed of the trolleybuses, led to a better service. A headway of 3 or 4 minutes became commonplace and on the 645 and 660 routes there was a trolleybus every 1 or 2 minutes at peak times. One criticism levelled at the new buses concerned their carrying capacity. The Feltham trams had allowed twenty standing passengers, ten in each vestibule, so they could comfortably carry eighty-eight or more passengers; trolleybuses, with only five standing, were limited to seventy-five. Nevertheless, the trolleybus was noted for being able to shift crowds quickly; this was particularly noticeable at football grounds like Tottenham where crowds of 60,000 could be cleared by fleets of trolleybuses in around 50 minutes. Even at non-league Barnet (then called Barnet Alston, after the engineering firm in Alston Road) trolleybuses played a great part in transporting the crowd to Underhill. In 1938 and 1939 when the famous Barnet Fair arrived in September, so great was the attraction that trolleybuses on the 609 would often be full by the time they reached Holloway Road on their journey northward.

The new trolleybuses were handsome vehicles. The red livery was broken by a broad cream band along the sides just below the saloon windows with a narrower cream band between decks. Initially they had silver roofs but these were painted brown during the war to lessen their visibility from the air and this was retained thereafter. A special logo, incorporating the LT roundel, a large letter T and the word 'Trolleybus' appeared on the front of each vehicle and again on the lower rear window. Initially, a smaller version of the logo also appeared next to the entrance, to warn boarding passengers, but this was later dispensed with.

Although trolleybuses were good-looking vehicles, the interiors were somewhat spartan compared with the Feltham trams and, indeed, motor buses of the time. Inside, the downstairs side panels were brown rexine and the seats were covered in green moquette with green rexine on the backs. Upstairs the colour scheme was blue: the rexine on the side panels was blue and the moquette was blue too. The single-skinned ceilings on both decks were white, which gave them rather a cold appearance, although those on the upper deck would turn a dull yellow with time, thanks to the combined effects of cigarette, cigar and pipe smoke. The half-drop windows on both decks were opened by pinching a clip and pulling down, rather than winding a handle. The walls of the platform were predominantly of brown rexine and the grab poles were covered in a white plastic-type material. In later years all the seats, both upstairs and down, were recovered in green moquette and the side panels upstairs were recovered in brown rexine.

The plain upper deck of a trolleybus. Bare bulbs and pinch grip half-drop windows were strictly functional. (Author)

The Trolleybus logo alongside the platform was later dropped. (Author)

A hangover from tram days was the carrying of Metropolitan Stage Carriage plates on each trolleybus. These were oval enamel plates, each with its own unique number in large black letters and surmounted by a crown, and they were to be found low down on the bulkhead, just to the left of the platform. At one time all public service vehicles had to carry such plates but the requirement for motor buses to display them was subsequently dropped in 1939, when paper PSV licence discs were displayed instead and only trams, trolleybuses and taxis continued to be required to do so; London taxicabs still carry them. Unlike other London Transport buses, in the early days trolleybuses did not carry a depot code. This was a metal stencil plate which was positioned at waist level just behind the driver's cab on both the near and offside of the vehicle; each depot had a code (Colindale was CE, Finchley was FY, Highgate was HT and Stonebridge Park was SE) and there was another stencil plate alongside which carried the vehicle's running number for that day. Depot plates were not introduced on trolleybuses until 1950.

The three-axle design was forced upon London Transport, and indeed other trolleybus operators, because the Construction and Use Regulations introduced under the Road Traffic Act of 1930 allowed maximum dimensions for buses of 27ft 6in long and 7ft 6in wide for a vehicle with two axles. The length could be extended to 30ft if the vehicle had three axles, so this was the only option if high-capacity vehicles were required. Later on restrictions were lifted, but trolleybuses continued to be built in the same form right up to the end. London Transport actually used a motor bus chassis (the AEC Renown, which was used on single-deck LT buses) as a basis for their trolleybuses.

Although one of the main reasons for the introduction of trolleybuses as replacement for trams was the existence of a large amount of expensive infrastructure, it was necessary to make alterations to accommodate the new vehicles. In particular new wiring had to be installed; trolleybuses required both a positive and a negative wire, the latter being installed on the pavement side. New traction standards had to be erected to take the heavier wiring and soon these dark green poles spaced 120ft apart became part of the everyday scene. As with the trams, Board of Trade regulations required the overhead to be divided into sections about half a mile in length, each section being separated by a wooden insulator and controlled by a dark green section box sited on the pavement. This allowed for the sections to be isolated in the event of accidents or for maintenance of the wires. White bands painted on the traction poles at the start of a section warned trolleybus drivers to ease off the power to prevent dewirements. Because the former LCC conduit tram routes had never required overhead wires and their consequent traction poles, these had to be installed before trolleybuses could run.

Everyone who used trolleybuses would remember the occasional dewirements, when the trolley arms would become separated from the wires and the conductor (or driver, if there was a conductress on board) would reach under the bus for the long bamboo pole which was kept in a tube under the bus. This would be used to reattach the trolley heads back onto the overhead, or sometimes to relocate them onto another set of wires. Drivers who failed to check their vehicles before setting out from the depot would sometimes find that they were minus a pole, in which case they would have to wait for the following bus and use theirs. A really resourceful driver would purloin a pole from another bus at the depot before setting off.

At some busy junctions a pole would be attached to a traction standard which could be used in emergencies. Because of the more physical nature of a trolleybus crew's duties, slightly different standards were applied to their recruitment. Drivers had to be between twenty-six and thirty-four years old and conductors between twenty-three and twenty-eight and the minimum height was 5ft 8in, compared with 5ft 7in for motor bus crews.

At intersections, or where one route diverged from another, the junction was controlled by 'frogs' on the overhead which performed the same function as points on a railway. When a bus reached such a junction the conductor would jump off the platform and pull a handle mounted on a traction standard which would set the correct route. Depending on the location in some cases it was merely necessary to pull the handle and then release it, in others the handle had to be held down until the bus had passed. Conductors usually performed this duty with consummate ease, but woe betide the man or woman who got it wrong; the bus would be dewired in the middle of a busy junction and the bamboo pole would have to come to the rescue. What was even worse was if this happened on a dead section, the trolleybus would become marooned in a sea of traffic and would either have to use its batteries to get to a live section or, if these were not working, it would have to be pushed. On a round trip on route 621 (North Finchley to Holborn) the conductor would have to pull the frogs no less than six times.

Left: An idea of the complexity and unsightliness of the overhead wiring can be seen in this view at Nag's Head, Holloway. (Fred Ivey)

Below left: At St Gabriel's Church, Cricklewood, the crew of trolleybus 1636 are in real trouble. Not only has one of the booms become dewired, but it has been bent in the process. The vehicle would have had to have been towed back to the depot. (Fred Ivey)

Below: The bamboo pole was kept in a tube running underneath the trolleybus. (Author)

The smooth and rapid acceleration of the trolleybus was due, in part, to its controls. Rather than the speed being increased by operation of a controller, the trolleybus driver achieved acceleration and braking by the use of foot pedals, in much the same way as a conventional bus. The left-hand pedal not only acted as accelerator but also a brake; easing off the power kicked in the regenerative braking and the right-hand pedal operated the air brake which finally brought the vehicle to a halt. Regenerative braking not only saved electricity but also reduced wear on tyres and brakes. Tram conductors who had transferred to trolleybuses took some time to get accustomed to the new vehicles; whereas on the trams they knew when the motorman was about to brake as they could hear the click as he eased off the power, but with trolleybuses there was no such warning. The trolleybus driver's worst fear, that the booms would become detached from the overhead wires, would instantly be confirmed when an orange neon light above his windscreen was extinguished; this meant that there had been a loss of power.

Because of the risk of dewirements, trolleybus drivers needed a special skill that was not needed for tram or motor bus drivers: they had to concentrate not just on the road ahead and on other traffic but also on the overhead wires. In order to help them steer the right path they would get into the habit of using features such as manhole covers and irregularities in the road surface to line themselves up correctly. This trick was, of course, particularly important at junctions where they needed to execute right or left turns.

With the inability of trolleybuses to overtake each other without lowering the booms and then reconnecting them, the sight of a long line of trolleybuses proceeding one after another became familiar on busy routes. As traffic increased over the years this sight became more familiar and was one reason why inspectors were employed on trolleybus routes to try and prevent bunching.

Finchley depot had room for 108 trolleybuses and it had the distinction of providing London's first trolleybus each day. This would leave the depot at 2.56a.m. and was particularly useful to people working in Fleet Street and at the Mount Pleasant sorting office, where workers had unsociable shifts. As well as these scheduled buses, Finchley also operated staff buses during the night. Although these were only intended to take LT staff between Finchley depot and Nag's Head, Holloway and Barnet and Cricklewood, they carried conductors and would stop at bus stops to pick up ordinary passengers. These buses did not feature on public timetables but night workers soon discovered their existence and used them regularly.

Finchley can claim the record of having the shortest-lived trolleybus route in London. The 651 was introduced on Sunday 6 March 1938, ran from Barnet Church to Golders Green and was extended during weekday off-peak times to Cricklewood. Only eighty-six days later, on Tuesday 31 May 1938, it was withdrawn. Passengers used the 645 instead, which had an increased frequency. Finchley depot also held another record: it was chosen to operate the first chassisless trolleybus in London, No.754. The 1930s were a fruitful period for bus designs; the LGOC had introduced the STL-type bus and the revolutionary side-engined Q-type in 1932 and London Transport produced the RT in 1939. Work started on designing a chassisless trolleybus in 1935 and its success lead to a further 177 being built and the experience gained from the experiment led eventually to the development of the Routemaster bus, which did not have a conventional chassis. Trolleybus No.754 had another distinction – it was the only one in the fleet to have a separate narrow exit door just behind the front nearside wheel and thus resembled the Feltham tram. The bus was withdrawn from service in March 1955.

There was one basic difference between trolleybuses and trams that necessitated some additional infrastructure work on the network. At a terminus, such as Barnet, trams would merely reverse, but trolleybuses were unable to do this, so wiring loops had to be constructed enabling them to turn round and return the way they had come from. At Barnet, LPTB wanted to construct a loop along Wood Street to the Black Horse Inn, returning through Union Street and the narrow portion of the High Street to the church. This was vehemently opposed by both Barnet Urban District Council and Hertfordshire County Council in 1936 and in the end a compromise was reached whereby the war memorial was moved some 36ft southwards on to a specially built island around which the trolleybuses could turn, but there was initially some opposition to this from the Barnet branch of the British Legion. An interesting aspect of this whole affair was the criticism heaped on Barnet UDC, who had prepared these plans in secret and had not mentioned them to the LPTB when their plans were in embryonic form; Barnet in fact waited until the necessary Bill was published and then presented a petition against it. An editorial in the *Barnet Press* summed it up thus: 'The Council has blundered, and the blunder is going to be costly, but that does not alter the fact that people who love their old town do not want to hasten the day when Barnet will be indistinguishable from Highgate or Tooting.'

Experimental chassisless trolleybus No.754 was the only one in the fleet to have a separate exit door. This was eventually locked and passengers only used the rear platform. The vehicle only operated from Finchley depot. (© TfL from the London Transport Museum Collection)

Above left: Trolleybus 754 shows off its innards. The Exit Only door can be seen on the left. (© TfL from the London Transport Museum Collection)

Above right: C2 trolleybus No.184 leaves the trolleybus station at Tally Ho. It would then turn right past the Gaumont Cinema and head down Ballards Lane towards Hammersmith. This particular vehicle was one of a batch that was instantly recognisable by the spats over the rear wheels. (Len Anderson)

Trolleybus crews were a tough breed. At Craven Park on 31 December 1961 the conductor of No.1636 on route 660 to Paddington struggles with the pole while No.1610 waits patiently for him to finish his work. (Fred Ivey)

This view from the top of Barnet Church in 1961 shows two trolleybuses on the stand. The blinds have already been altered for their return journeys; the 645 in front will be heading back to Canons Park and the 609 will later leave for Moorgate. The wires of the turning circle can clearly be seen in front of the smaller church roof. (Ron Kingdon)

At the Barnet terminus there was room for only two trolleybuses on the stand – a third trolleybus would have to park further down the hill. On one of the traction poles there was an illuminated display consisting of two lights. When a trolleybus left the stand, one of the lights would automatically be extinguished, thus giving authority for the last vehicle to move up to the stand. A relic of earlier times was a horse trough which was situated on the stepped pavement. There was also a small hut which contained a telephone for use by the inspectors.

A feature of the trolleybus system was the use of headway recording clocks which were sited on some twenty of LT's premises, ranging from trolleybus depots to Underground stations and also in the entrance hall at 55 Broadway, the LT headquarters. These devices were originally installed by MET in 1928 and they consisted of circular discs with the hours marked round the outside, like a clock face. Each trolleybus movement was recorded by a mark on the perimeter which would indicate the regularity of the services and would show where bunching was occurring. Information was gathered via skates on the overhead wires which would trip as each trolleybus passed. Skates were situated at Ballards Lane, at the bottom of Archway Road, Golders Green, and by St Michael's Church in Bounds Green Road. Two of the recording clocks were situated in Finchley depot.

Above left: Drama at North Finchley on 28 January 1961. The booms on trolleybus 1478 have become lodged on the span wires and No.1467 has had to lower its booms and proceed past it on battery power. (A.G. Newman)

Above right: Eventually a tower wagon has to be called in to sort out the problem, with help from a young policeman, two inspectors and a gang from Finchley depot. (A.G. Newman)

Trolleybus 1506 leaves the forecourt at Golders Green Station on its way to Barnet. (Fred Ivey)

At Holborn the problem of turning trolleybuses at the end of the route resulted in a special arrangement. Trolleybuses on routes 517 and 521 went down Caledonian Road then Gray's Inn Road along High Holborn and returned via Charterhouse Street, Farringdon Road and King's Cross. On route 617 and 621 the situation was reversed, the routing being Caledonian Road, Farringdon Road, Charterhouse Street and High Holborn and then northwards via Gray's Inn Road to Caledonian Road. Strangely enough, although trolleybuses went along High Holborn, they did not stop there as there were no bus stops for them. High Holborn was the nearest that trolleybuses reached to the centre of London; the LCC trams, even though they had discreet conduit, had never managed to penetrate into the West End and the City and the authorities were certainly never going to allow unsightly traction poles and overhead wires to detract from historic buildings. Further north, at East Finchley Station a special turning circle was erected in the forecourt by May 1941, although this was not often used. At the newly created terminus at Finsbury Square 85 trolleybuses an hour would arrive or depart at peak times. Two of the most heavily used junctions were at Nag's Head, Holloway Road and Manor House, both of which saw over 4,000 trolleybus movements a day. At the complicated Nag's Head junction over 1.5 tons of overhead wire was in place. The trolleybus station at Tally Ho was the only place on the system where routes from three different directions met and in rush hours fifty-eight vehicles an hour were using the station.

A trolleybus turns from Holborn into Gray's Inn Road on its return journey, having travelled to Holborn Circus via Farringdon Road. (Commercial postcard)

Although trolleybuses were not as flexible as motor buses, one of the features of their operation was the practice of turning them short of their destination in order to provide a better service when traffic congestion caused late running. Inspectors posted at turn round points would be constantly monitoring the running of trolleybuses and would instruct drivers to curtail their journeys and return to their original start point. Depending on the location, this would involve running around specially constructed turning circles (like the one at East Finchley Station), or dewiring and moving the booms to adjacent wires (as at New Southgate Station), or running round specially wired side roads to regain the main route. Perhaps one of the most unusual turn round points was just north of Henly's corner, where northbound trolleybuses on routes 645 and 660 would stop in Regent's Park Road, the trolley booms would be taken down and the bus would reverse on battery power into Fitzalan Road and then turn back into the main road, where the poles would be replaced on the southbound wires. This turning point was known as Holly Park and was carried on destination blinds; Holly Park is the road on the east of Regent's Park Road, nearly opposite Fitzalan Road and at the end of which the southbound trolleybuses would restart their journey.

Despite the best efforts of inspectors, there were still complaints about the service: Friern Barnet Council asked the LTE in 1948 to receive a deputation to register complaints about the 521 and 621 services. A leader in the *Finchley Press* of 6 February 1948 was equally scathing:

Why, oh! why, must these buses travel in bunches of three to six at a time? Is it that the drivers don't know the way and need a pathfinder? Or are they nervous wrecks incapable of independent action? Could it be that the highly placed (and, no doubt, highly paid) individuals responsible for arranging the timing schedules don't know their job? It is even possible that the more lowly placed (and, undoubtedly, less well paid) staff, who receive these schedules, regard them as pieces of paper, useful for personal memoranda and other purposes, and take no notice of them whatever.

Above left: The seldom-used turning circle at East Finchley Station. (Fred Ivey)

Above right: Trolleybus 1630 emerges from Fitzalan Road on battery power. (Fred Ivey)

Trolleybus 215 in a sorry state after its dramatic accident. (Barnet Press)

Accidents involving trolleybuses were comparatively few; however on Friday 31 December 1938 a trolleybus on route 609 from Barnet was involved in a nasty accident in Whetstone, just after Walfield Avenue. The bus skidded on the slippery road, lurched across the road and hit an oncoming Green Line coach. The trolleybus driver was thrown out of his cab and the driverless vehicle then collided with a fence outside number 1507 High Road. A 135 bus, which was following the Green Line northward, braked and was hit from behind by a van. Broken glass covered the roadway and the unfortunate trolleybus driver, Frank Ernest Skinner, lay in the roadway where he had been thrown. Several people were removed to Barnet Hospital for treatment: seven passengers on the trolleybus; the driver and conductor on the Green Line and three of their passengers; the bus driver and the van driver.

A truly spectacular accident occurred at 11.45a.m. on Monday 9 February 1948 at Hendon Aerodrome where an RAF Anson aircraft was trying to land on one engine as part of a training exercise. The pilot thought he saw an obstruction on the runway and decided to overshoot and come round again. He misjudged his height and collided with scaffolding surrounding newly constructed flats at Stag Lane, Burnt Oak Broadway. He missed the London Co-operative store, the Bald Faced Stag pub and the Stag House Civic Restaurant by a few yards but hit a trolleybus traction standard, which bent in two, and collided with a trolleybus, No.215, heading southwards on route 645. The aircraft then overturned and the pilot and co-pilot were killed but, miraculously, only nine passengers on the trolleybus were injured, none of them seriously. The driver, George Halsey, received a cut finger and, not surprisingly, suffered from severe shock. Local residents took the opportunity to lobby against continued flying from the aerodrome.

CHAPTER 12

THE WAR & AFTERWARDS

With the outbreak of the Second World War on Sunday 3 September 1939 the pattern of London's transport dramatically changed. The replacement of trams with trolleybuses in south London was put on hold and there were to be no new motor buses built until September 1941, when the Ministry of War Transport allowed the bodying of eleven Leyland TD7 chassis on which work had started but which had been stopped by the war.

The Government had introduced blackout regulations which meant that no lights were allowed to be shown at night and street lights were turned off, homes had blackout curtains or blinds fitted and vehicles were not allowed to use their lights. In the early years of the war careless householders could be fined as much as £2 for allowing lights to show at night and local newspapers carried reports of court cases as a deterrent to others. London Transport set about masking the headlights on all their vehicles, so that only a glimmer showed and initially bus blinds were unlit, although this was rescinded later. Lights in the interiors of buses and trams were severely masked to such an extent that it was almost impossible to read a newspaper and a conductor's job became much harder, with the necessity to issue the right tickets, punch them in the correct place and count the change in the gloom. Motor buses had a large white spot painted on their lower rear panels, where the advertisements used to be, as a warning to following traffic, but this was never applied to trolleybuses, as it might have encouraged them to overtake each other at night and become dewired in the process. Ron Kingdon, an employee of Northmet, the electricity undertaking, recalled that they were issued with special identity cards, complete with a photograph, as their duties would entail them entering the premises of other public utilities. On one occasion during May 1940 he and another electrician, Frank Murray, were instructed to go to Finchley depot and erect blackout material over the fanlights high up in the roof spaces. They managed this with two long ladders, blackout paper, chicken wire, laths and luck and daring. It was hot and dusty up among the rafters, but they were getting time-and-a-half after 12.30p.m.! Ron remembers watching the trolleybuses coming and going down below as they held the material in place with long-handled brooms (an arm-aching job) and their only protection was a cloth cap. Fortunately, the staff at the depot kept them supplied with refreshments.

In the early days of the war the threat of invasion was taken very seriously and London Transport posted armed guards at all their garages, including Finchley depot. Staff had to show their National Registration Identity Cards and Staff Pass and failure to do so could have been fatal, as the guards had orders to fire on anyone not obeying their instructions.

Fuel, including electricity for trams and trolleybuses, was at a premium and passengers were urged only to use public transport if they had to. Posters carried slogans such as 'Is Your Journey

Really Necessary?'; 'Don't Ride for Fun Unless Your Fun is Work' and 'Walk Short Distances and Leave Room for Those Who Have Longer Journeys'. LPTB managed to secure economies in fuel and rubber either by resiting some bus stops or by removing some altogether.

One important regulation that was introduced was the previously unheard of system of queuing. The quaintly named Regulation of Traffic (Formation of Queues) Order of 1942 made it mandatory to form a queue, two abreast, at bus stops where six or more people were waiting; this was necessary because the reduced frequency of many services led to big build ups of passengers. Failure to observe this byelaw could lead to a fine not exceeding 40s (£2). Steel bus shelters were also introduced at key locations and these served not only to keep some of the queue dry in wet weather but also had the psychological effect of making them feel less vulnerable to air raids. In the early days of the war people would take cover at the sound of every air-raid warning but eventually they became more blasé and continued about their business; when the V2s started arriving in 1944 there was very little warning anyway. During the whole of the war London Transport lost only fifteen trolleybuses and none of these was from Finchley depot.

Whilst there were numerous temporary interruptions or curtailment to trolleybus services due to damage to the overhead, these were usually quickly repaired. The most serious transport-related incident in the area occurred at Bounds Green Underground Station on Saturday 13 October 1940 when a bomb fell on to the westbound platform, killing nineteen people who were sheltering there, and injuring fifty-two. The station remained closed until 10 December 1940.

Trolleybuses wait at Charterhouse Street for the return journey to North Finchley. The white-painted mudguards and masked headlamps were introduced in the Blackout. (© TfL from the London Transport Museum Collection)

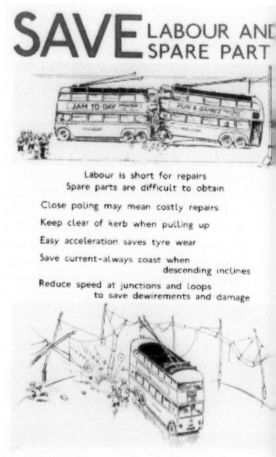

Above left: During the war women took over many of the jobs previously held by men. Two ladies pause for a photograph before continuing cleaning a trolleybus at Wood Green depot. The blind of this bus carries the unusual destination of Wood Green Station – the usual description was just Wood Green. (Lyn Barclay)

Above right: Poster from 1942. (© TfL from the London Transport Museum Collection)

One problem shared by both trams and trolleybuses was the question of arcing which produced vivid flashes at certain junctions and under certain conditions. Where feasible, hoods were placed above the overhead wires at such junctions and drivers were warned to avoid causing arcing at all costs. All vehicles were restricted to 20mph which played havoc with schedules, but schedules had been amended anyway, with many services severely curtailed after 8p.m. Although many motor bus routes were amended or curtailed, trolleybuses were generally not too affected as, of course, it was difficult to divert them without erecting new overhead. The opening of the Northern Line extension to High Barnet on Sunday 14 April 1940 helped to take some of the strain off trolleybus route 609.

The Government introduced Double Summer Time which somewhat relieved the situation during the months of May to August, but the winter months still presented problems to drivers. One measure to try and improve visibility at night was the painting of kerbs, traffic islands, and even trees, with white paint. All LT vehicles had the leading edge of their front mudguards painted white and the edges of their platforms were similarly treated. At New Southgate small 'fairy lights' were strung on the overhead wires at the sharp turn from Friern Barnet Road into Station Road and reflective road studs were installed in the carriageway in 1940.

With the coming of the Blitz in September 1940, new hazards emerged for passengers and crews. The danger of flying glass was dealt with by applying netting to the insides of all non-opening windows on buses and trolleybuses. A small diamond was left clear through which passengers could peer and passengers and conductors helped each other by calling out destinations. Opening windows were not treated but they carried labels with instructions to open the windows in air raids to lessen the effect of blast. Trolleybus breakdown crews were unable to work at night but repairs were usually effected within 4 hours during the following day. LT were sometimes able to report air-raid damage even before ARP personnel on the ground because they were able to tell from the loss of power where an incident had occurred.

Although people had been prepared to accept the difficulties that affected everyone in the early stages of the war, towards the end they were becoming more critical. Friern Barnet UDC had written to LPTB in January 1945 to complain about the irregularity of timing on routes 521 and 621 and in its reply, LPTB stated that its inspectors had been instructed to endeavour to ensure even running but manpower shortage, absence through sickness and adverse weather conditions made it difficult to immediately fill the gaps. The council reluctantly decided that no further action could be taken but they would monitor the situation.

The immediate post-war period was one of extreme austerity and shortage of all goods was common; even bread was rationed, something that had never occurred even during the darkest days of the war. To make things worse, the winter of 1947 was the harshest since 1881, with freezing temperatures and heavy snowfalls. The snow started falling on Friday 24 January and it snowed every day until 16 March. Shortages of fuel led to power cuts and Standard and Telephones and Cables at New Southgate had to lay off over 5,000 (only the 2,000 office staff were retained) and they were joined by over 1,000 staff at the other big employer in the area, John Dale's, where machinery was at a standstill. Street lights were turned off and only traffic lights and obelisks remained lit; ladies' hairdressers cancelled all appointments where electricity was required. Needless to say, the trolleybus network, indeed all public transport, was hugely affected, but people were only travelling if they absolutely had to.

On Thursday 1 January 1948 the LPTB was replaced by the London Transport Executive (LTE) but it was business as usual and trolleybuses throughout London were responsible for 909 million passenger journeys during the first year of LTE's stewardship. On Sunday 1 October 1950 the Tram and Trolleybus Department ceased to exist and trolleybuses and trams came under the jurisdiction of the Central Bus Department of LTE. This meant that certain long-established practices were immediately curtailed to bring operation into line with that of motor buses: inspectors were no longer allowed to switch trolleybuses from one route to another to maintain an even service; this inevitably led to a poorer service. Workmen tickets were immediately withdrawn, to be replaced

Bell Punch tickets like these had been in use on trams, buses and trolleybuses from the early 1900s. (Author)

by early morning single fares (2d instead of the normal 1s1d) which applied before 8a.m. In 1938 it had been calculated that of some 400 million trolleybus journeys, 60 million (or 15 per cent) of them were on workmen's tickets, so this represented quite a sizeable chunk of revenue. In 1949 the London Transport Executive commissioned the *London Travel Survey* from Research Services Ltd which, amongst other things, showed that 47 per cent of workers started work before 8a.m. and 49 per cent of them finished between 4.45 and 5.30p.m.; the scope for staggering working hours was therefore huge and the Ministry of Transport backed a campaign to try and get passengers to avoid the evening peak times.

The 1950s saw the departure of an old friend – the Bell Punch ticket machine and the rack of individual and colourful pre-printed tickets that had been carried by tram, bus and trolleybus conductors since the early 1900s. Its replacement was the Gibson machine, named after its inventor George Gibson who worked at London Transport's Punch Works in Brixton. The Gibson carried a roll of blank paper upon which a whole range of tickets could be printed; this speeded up the ticket-issuing process and each machine recorded the number and value of tickets issued. In Bell Punch days, each machine punched a hole in a ticket with a melodious 'ting' and the tiny circle of coloured paper was retained in the machine. In the event of any queries, it was the unbelievable task of some unfortunate person to count each and every one of these, from which a record of the day's transactions could be obtained.

CHAPTER 13
TROLLEYBUS MEMORIES

A North Finchley resident, Richard Testar, who lived in Torrington Park and started school at Haberdashers in 1955, recalled his daily journeys on the 645 and the 660:

I normally got the 660 from the Gaumont, North Finchley but sometimes I caught a 645 from the stop outside Jones the Bakers at the top of Torrington Park. With much less traffic in those days I was able to catch the 8.15 from the depot and still get to school at 8.55. This was usually a 645, which had terminated at Tally Ho and was on its way back to Colindale. I remember the overhead rumble as the trolley went under the points, and how there was often a load of sparks if the driver didn't lift his foot off the power pedal when it went over those special joins in the wiring at various intervals.

The bus usually filled up fast; sometimes it was full by Granville Road and it really belted down to Finchley Central, which you couldn't do nowadays! It often had a non-stop run at a good speed between The Queens Head at East End Road and Henly's Corner because it was always full by then and no-one wanted to get off until the Naked Lady at the North Circular. There is a fairly steep hill from Henly's Corner up to the top of Temple Fortune and I can recall how fast the acceleration was if it pulled away from a stop on the hill. If it moved off behind an RT on route 102 it used to zip round it as if it was turbo-charged. Golders Green was where many people piled on and off. I remember there was a turning crescent just after the station, where the 102 buses terminated. There was also provision for a trolleybus turnaround but I don't remember it being used much. From Golders Green it was off to Child's Hill where the trolleybus competed with routes 2, 2a, 2b, 13 and 28.

There was a sharp right-hand turn at Child's Hill into Cricklewood Lane where the driver obviously took it carefully in case it came off the wires. The first part of Cricklewood Lane was very steep and I can remember my first crash! A car pulled out from a turning on the left and the trolleybus skidded into it (I think it was a wet road). Nobody was hurt but we were all turned off and the arms and the trolley poles were taken down with the bamboo pole which was stored under the bus. We all poured off at Westbere Road opposite Cricklewood Station.

On the return journey it was useful to get a 645 as it took me one stop further. At 4.10p.m. there was always a throng of Habs' boys waiting at the stop. Funnily enough, whilst we are often appalled at the behaviour of schoolchildren these days, we all seemed just as rowdy then. Often the trolleybus would come from under the railway bridge and, although obviously half empty, would see the rabble, sail past the stop and ignore us. We all booed and shouted at the driver to no avail. I don't remember, however, any 'f' words, which you would hear these days. Perhaps it was because Haberdashers purported to be a public school! At the Gaumont, North Finchley, the 645s went on to Barnet and the 660s turned right onto the bus station. This meant that the conductor had to get off the 660 and pull a brass handle to change the points. Sometimes we did it for him as we jumped off, but I do recall one occasion when a schoolmate pretended to pull the handle, resulting in the arms coming off the wires as it turned into the station. We all ran!

If the conductor was upstairs at the front, where there was no bell or buzzer he (or she) would give the starting signal by either stamping on the floor twice or by bashing the bulkhead with his ticket rack. If the conductor was at the rear upstairs he or she would peer into the round mirror which gave a view of the platform. Three rings on the bell by the conductor indicated to the driver that the bus was full and he need not stop at the next one. Forgetting school days for a moment, I must have been about seven or eight, and I can remember the terminus at Barnet Church. There was room for only two trolleybuses at the stand, but as the terminus couldn't be seen from the lower stop there was a light system on a pole outside Caney's the flower shop just down the hill and opposite the Police Station. There were two lighted strips in a glass panel; when the first bus moved off from the terminal it extinguished one of the lights, indicating that a space was available. Very ingenious for those days! However, better than that and before the light system was introduced, an inspector would position himself outside the Terminus Snack Bar opposite the Red Lion as it then was. He then had a view of both the terminus and the lower stop and when there was a vacancy on the stand he would blow a shrill whistle to tell the waiting bus down the hill that it could move up to the terminus. There was often an LT man who used to sit on a stool by the side of the Gaumont in Kingsway, North Finchley. He would be ready to pull a handle mounted on a traction pole to change the points for the 609 to go on to Barnet and save the conductor having to jump out into a busy road.

Inspectors were responsible for ensuring that the best possible service was achieved on all routes and to do this they had to have a detailed knowledge of the geography of the route; the time schedules, including headways and running times; the duty rosters of the drivers and conductors, including meal reliefs; and special characteristics of each route, for example factories, sports grounds, schools etc. which could all result in extra demand at certain times. When they needed to curtail a service short of its destinations they would have to supervise the transfer of passengers on to the following vehicle.

On the subject of inspectors, Gwen Dow's husband, Martin, was a Gold Badge Inspector based at Wood Green Garage and his area included Finchley, Barnet, Wood Green, Golders Green and Palmers Green. Gwen recalled how conscientious he was. Martin and Gwen would travel all over London by bus on his days off and, whilst he had a pass allowing free travel, Gwen had to pay her own fares. Martin would give her the money before they boarded the bus and he would then sit apart from her. Only after she had paid her fare to the conductor would Martin move and sit beside her for the rest of the journey. Martin, who came from Glasgow, was known to the trolleybus crews as 'Indicator Jock' because of his insistence that the destination blinds were correctly set before allowing the buses to leave the terminus.

Trolleybus 1589 emerges from under the bridge at the bottom of Barnet Hill. (Ron Kingdon)

At the county boundary a trolleybus sweeps past the last steam–driven road roller to work in the Barnet area. The sign on the lamppost that reads 'Keep Well to the Left' has been carefully turned round so that it does not contradict the temporary 'Keep Right' sign. (Ron Kingdon)

Jock was commended by London Transport for bravery when in March 1976 a bomb exploded on a Piccadilly Line train on the northbound platform at Wood Green Station. Jock and a fellow inspector, Bob Sheffield, were on duty at Spouters Corner, Wood Green, and they reacted promptly to the emergency. Jock rushed down the escalator onto the platform which was full of acrid smoke and dust and found a man badly cut by flying glass. Whilst he was bringing him to the surface Bob was telephoning 999 and taking the name and addresses of other injured passengers. Without a second thought, Jock returned to the platform and shepherded the remaining passengers from the scene. When the police arrived Jock and Bob went off to resume their regular duties.

Ron Kingdon, who was a keen bus photographer, recalls that Jock would very kindly position the trolleybuses for the best position for his photos. On the last day of trolleybus operation, Jock lined up the crew of the last trolleybus for a final photograph at Barnet.

Another local resident, Joyce Robinson, recalls that her father was an Inspector at Finchley depot until his retirement in 1967, having worked for London Transport since 1936. Charles Arthur King started as a conductor on the trams and then became a motorman. During the war Joyce recalls her father coming home and telling her that he had been sent home because there was an unexploded bomb at the depot which was subsequently defused by a courageous member of the bomb squad, accompanied by a secretary who sat on the edge of the crater and took notes. They later heard that the pair had been killed in another incident.

Trolleybus 312 is about to be overtaken by a Bedford lorry carrying what looks like a potentially unsafe load in this view from 1959 in Ballards Lane. An inspector awaits the next northbound bus. (Fred Ivey)

Joyce remembers a curious incident during the Blitz. Her father was passing a junction box in Woodhouse Road and heard an unusual humming noise; he reported this back at the depot but nobody could explain why this should be. The same thing happened the following evening and this time he mentioned it to an engineer who thought that the cause could be interference from a radio transmitter. These incidents coincided with strange goings on at Charles's house in Hollickwood Avenue which backed on to Coppetts Wood. One night his wife, on her way to the Anderson shelter in the garden with the children, had heard footsteps from the next door garden and she called out 'Goodnight' to her neighbour, but received no reply. The same thing occurred the next night and, on asking her neighbour why she had not replied, she was told that she had not been there. Charles reported to the police at New Southgate who suggested that they put a watering can on the path and see if anyone removed it. Sure enough, the next morning it had been moved and the back garden gate was ajar. Joyce vividly recalls that the next evening a fat policemen was sitting in their hallway and she was told that he was conducting surveillance, presumably looking out for someone who was hiding in the wood. Much later the police told them that they had shadowed a man all the way to Manchester and he was subsequently hanged at Strangeways Prison. This could, of course, be propaganda by the authorities but the case of the buzzing junction box is one that has, as far as she knew, not been solved.

Joyce recalls that each Christmas the children of the staff were invited to a party in Finchley depot at which they were given small bags of sweets that had somehow been accumulated during the year, despite the severe rationing.

Another incident from the Second World War gives a good illustration of just how conscientious trolleybus people were. Mrs I. Dawson recalled:

> One evening Mother and I were in the house next-door to our own home in Woodhouse Road. There was an air raid going on and we were all worried and quiet. Suddenly there was a big knock at the front door; it was my father, he was a trolleybus driver. He had stopped his bus outside the house and asked if he could bring in his passengers, as it was a bad raid and all were worried. In they all came and the conductress too. We noticed that she looked more upset than the other people, and asked her why. She told us she had left her two children alone in the house; she was very upset. The raid being over in due course, they all departed to the bus. We heard afterwards that the children were all right. My father was not supposed to leave his bus, but he thought of his passengers.

Until 1956, when the Clean Air Act was introduced, smogs had been a regular feature of London winters. The fog was yellow with sulphur and visibility would be so poor that it was possible to get lost just crossing the road from one side to the other; footsteps were almost inaudible and people would suddenly loom out of the fog without warning. The winter of 1952 was the worst on record with over 4,000 dying of respiratory diseases. In common with other inspectors and conductors, Joyce's father would have to walk in front of the trolleybuses at Barnet Church carrying a flare to guide them. At certain points where there was a sharp bend in the road, New Southgate being one, a series of light bulbs were strung from the overhead and these 'fairy lights', as they were nicknamed, helped to guide trolleybus drivers in poor visibility.

Yvonne Ruge, who was a pupil at Woodhouse School in the late 1950s, recalls the frequency with which the buses would become dewired on the long curve of Woodhouse Road outside the school. The resulting struggle the conductor had with the bamboo pole lightened many bored hours at the first floor library windows and proved a welcome distraction to Latin lessons.

Local resident Shirley Gardiner recalls that boarding a trolleybus at Wood Green Station in the rush hour was a 'circus act'. Just as everyone had scrambled on board:

> Whoosh – we were off, a few of us still on the platform swaying about and trying to get our balance. I'll never know how the trolley took off so quickly up Jolly Butchers Hill with so much power. The allotted number of passengers standing holding on to the rails swayed about, sometimes falling on to those seated or even treading on their toes.

Ron Kingdon remembers trolleybus conductors (and tram conductors before them) calling out 'The Naked Lady' when they reached the statute of La Deliverance in Regents Park Road and 'Have your passports ready' as they approached Golders Green!

Boxing Day in 1961 and there are few passengers in High Road, Whetstone, for trolleybus No.1581. The Green Line bus stop can be seen further up on the left. (Ron Kingdon)

On a winter's day the interior of trolleybus 1488 glows invitingly as it proceeds carefully down Barnet Hill on route 645 to Golders Green. (Ron Kingdon)

Although they were quiet, the trolleybuses did have noises of their own. There was the gentle whine of the motors and, for passengers sitting in the seats behind the driver, the clicking sound of the contactors as the bus accelerated. Upstairs there was a rumbling caused by the booms. Even the sound of the bell was unlike that of a motor bus, it did not have their resonant ring, but was somehow more muffled. In the lower saloon a bell cord ran most of the length of the gangway, on the nearside. Youngsters would delight in announcing the approach of a trolleybus even before it came into view by pressing an ear to a traction pole and listening for the sound of the booms which was transmitted along the overhead wires. The wires themselves would start to sway as a trolleybus approached.

Trolleybuses came under the jurisdiction of the Tram Department of the LPTB and consequently some of the tram practices were carried over to trolleybuses. Perhaps the most obvious were the route and destination blinds which had distinctive numbering and lettering, quite unlike those of motor buses. Trolleybus blinds were prepared at Charlton works (bus blinds were made at Chiswick) and they were less informative, having far fewer intermediate points, and sometimes none at all, merely a final destination. After 1950, when they came under the control of the Central Bus Department, they at least started to carry the familiar Johnston typeface, but they never altered that much. In 1952, with the opening of Aldenham bus overhaul works, trolleybus route and destination blinds were produced there. Another tram practice that was continued was the use of the word 'workman' on blinds; this would appear in place of the final destination on the rear destination box and after 8a.m., when workmen's fares ceased, the final destination would be shown again.

CHAPTER 14
THE END

London Transport's Annual Review of 1957 contained the following paragraph relating to trolleybuses:

> The Routemaster bus has been designed to replace the trolleybuses which (except for those in the Kingston area) must soon be replaced because of their age and condition. The decision to develop the Routemaster instead of ordering more trolleybuses was taken because, while there is little to choose between the two vehicles in costs of operation, the trolleybus is at a disadvantage compared with the bus on other important grounds: trolleybuses cannot overtake each other, so that if one is delayed, it holds back those following; mass hold-ups may occur through de-wirements or power failures; and trolleybuses cannot easily be diverted when a road is under repair, or when traffic demand shifts from one district to another. The oil bus, with its independent power unit, is much more flexible, not only in day-to-day operation but also in enabling services to be readily adapted to meet longer-term changes in traffic demand; it can also be concentrated much more easily to meet exceptional surges in traffic as, for example, at sporting events.

The changes that had taken place in society since the war had a considerable effect on public transport. Until the early 1950s people had higher wages but little to spend them on (rationing was still in force until 1954) which meant that there was more disposable income to spend on leisure, and public transport was the only way for most of the population to get to places of interest. The demand for cars started in 1950 and it was so great that manufacturers were unable to meet it. At this time the price of a second-hand car was actually greater than a new one (for example, in the July 1950 *Glass's Guide* a new Ford Anglia had a list price of £329 but the used retail price was £545). By the late fifties cars were becoming more readily available and the decline in public transport was rapid. In 1953 there were 747 million trolleybus journeys in London; by 1958 this had reduced to 477 million, a dramatic 36 per cent reduction. The introduction of a comfortable, modern motor bus with such luxuries as heating and good suspension might just, it was hoped, lure people back from the cars. The Routemaster was an undoubted success (it lasted forty-six years after all) but it was destined never to take the place of the car and the freedom that it offered.

1957 was the year after Suez and petrol was still rationed. It is easy with hindsight to think that the interruption of oil supplies might have been a warning to transport experts and that they should have considered that rising oil prices might have been a factor worth considering. However, the Routemaster was in the later stages of development (it would enter service in 1959) and it was clearly an excellent replacement for trolleybuses, so it is not surprising that the elderly trolleybus network was considered not worthy of further investment; eventually the Routemaster went on to replace motor buses as well. LTs calculations showed that there was, in fact, very little difference in the annual costs of running trolleybuses and motor buses, but the argument in favour of the increased flexibility of motor buses won the day.

To make matters even worse, there was a prolonged bus strike in London in 1958, lasting from 5 May to 20 June. During the seven weeks no buses or trolleybuses ran and by the time the strike was over many of LTE's passengers had learned how to manage without them. It was a blow that LTE was never to recover from and the decline continued thereafter.

Bus routes were curtailed and services reduced, which only exacerbated the situation. The withdrawal of trolleybuses in London was, like their introduction in the 1930s, done in stages; starting on Wednesday 4 March 1959 routes were withdrawn at approximately three-monthly intervals. Yellow notices headed 'Buses for Trolleybuses' were pasted on traction poles advising passengers of the new bus routes which would take over, and notices were placed in the local newspapers.

With a little help from Mr Chad, the motor industry took advantage of the 1958 bus strike.

On the last trolleybus to leave Barnet, Inspector Jock Dow relaxes, complete with leather gloves to keep out the bitter cold. (Ron Kingdon)

Although all the trolleybus routes in the area had been introduced on Sundays, they were all subsequently withdrawn on Tuesdays. The 517 and 617 (North Finchley to Holborn Circus via Highgate) last operated on 1 February 1961 and were replaced by bus route 17; the 521 and 621 (North Finchley to Holborn Circus via Wood Green) ceased on 7 November 1961 and were replaced by bus route 221 and the 609 (Moorgate–Barnet) was replaced by the 104 on the same day. On 3 January 1962 the 645 (Canons Park–Barnet) was replaced by the 245 and the 660 (North Finchley–Hammersmith) by the 260. A unique feature of the 609 withdrawal was that between April and November 1961 new Routemaster buses and trolleybuses jointly operated on this route on Sundays; this was the only occasion where Routemasters ran on a trolleybus-numbered route. Highgate depot, which had been supplying trolleybuses buses for the Sunday 609 service, had already been converted to Routemaster-only operation and was therefore unable to utilise trolleybuses.

This last withdrawal was memorable for at least one reason: the weather. On New Year's Eve 1961 there was a very heavy fall of snow in London and the Home Counties. On the last day of operation trolleybuses were proceeding gingerly up and down Barnet Hill on their last journeys and only the hardiest of enthusiasts were there to see their last journeys. Nevertheless, enthusiasts ensured that the trolleybuses had a good send off. The last 609 trolleybus (No.1513) left Barnet at 11.51p.m. on Tuesday 7 November and the last 645 (No.1564) left Barnet on Tuesday 2 January 1962 at 11.43p.m. The very last trolleybus to enter Finchley depot was No.1468 (an L3 class) on route 660.

A group of enthusiasts brave the snow and ice for a last picture at Barnet. (Ron Kingdon)

Trolleybuses awaiting scrapping in the yard behind Colindale depot in August 1962. Whilst some of the once-proud kings of the road made it under their own power, others suffered the ignominy of being towed there, as the chalked notice in the back window of K1 class No.1057 indicates. (Ron Kingdon)

For some years after their demise, traces of the trolleybuses could still been seen. Although most of the traction standards had been removed soon after the trolleybuses ceased to run, there were still a few which acted as lamp standards or telephone cable supports. A survey undertaken in 1978 by Mr B.L. Wibberley MSc, CEng, MIM, on behalf of the Hendon & District Archaeological Society found that in the section of Woodhouse Road from Summers Lane through to Station Road, New Southgate no fewer than thirty-one poles were still in use. Perhaps the most interesting of these were three poles situated in Friern Barnet Road outside the grounds of Friern Hospital (formerly Colney Hatch Lunatic Asylum) which still had the spiked 'dog collars' on them. These had been installed in tram days in an attempt to deter passers by from peering over the walls at the inmates and were known to trolleybus crews as 'lunatic spikes'.

Shortly after this survey was conducted, the poles were removed and replaced by concrete lamp standards. And so the last vestiges of the era of electric traction vanished forever.

Nowadays of course, the question of pollution-free transport is high on the agenda and has led to the reintroduction of tram systems in Croydon, Notttingham, Manchester and the West Midlands; and trolleybuses quite comfortably run in cities such as Vancouver and Zurich whilst in 2005 in Rome they reintroduced trolleybuses after a period of thirty-three years without them. If trolleybuses were running in London today, would a decision be made to abandon them in favour of diesel buses?

At Finchley depot in January 1961 a Scammell tractor from George Cohen's 600 Group prepares to tow away trolleybus No.1044 while RT 517 from Muswell Hill garage lays over. (Fred Ivey)

The future is represented by Routemaster RM 713 outside the gates of Friern Hospital in October 1972 on route 221 which replaced trolleybus routes 521 and 621. A trolleybus standard, complete with 'lunatic spikes' and street light can be seen near the entrance. (Jim Blake, North London Transport Society)

APPENDIX 1

TRAM & TROLLEYBUS CHRONOLOGY

Items in **bold** relate to the geographical area covered by this book.

1871   – North Metropolitan Tramways opens horse-drawn tram line from Finsbury Square to Nag's Head Holloway.

1872   – Line from Nag's Head Holloway is extended to Archway Tavern.

1875   – London Street Tramways opens horse-drawn tram line from Kentish Town to Archway Tavern.

1889   – LCC is formed and takes over tram operations.

1898   – On 13 May the first electric tramway in London opens in Alexandra Palace but closes on 30 September 1899.

1899   – The LCC opens its first tram line, in South London.

1901   – On 4 April LUT introduces the first electric trams in London, on the Shepherds Bush–Acton route.

1902   – **In October a contract is awarded for construction of a line between Highgate and Whetstone.**

1904   – On 22 July MET opens a line between Finsbury Park and Seven Sisters Corner and a line between Manor House and Three Jolly Butchers at Wood Green.
         – On 20 August MET opens a line between Wood Green and Bruce Grove Station.
         – On 3 December MET opens a line between Cricklewood and Hendon.
         – In December MET opens a tram depot at Hendon, between The Greenway and Annesley Avenue.

1905   – On 31 March MET opens a line between Cricklewood and Craven Park.
         – **On 16 May the LCC places a contract with Dick, Kerr to build line a between Archway and Archway Tavern.**
         – **On 7 June the MET opens the line between Highgate Archway and Whetstone.**
         – On 19 July MET opens a line between Angel Bridge, Edmonton and Tramway Avenue.
         – **In August the Archway–Archway Tavern line is completed but not opened.**
         – **In November the Middlesex County Council decides to extend the line from Totteridge northwards to the Middlesex–Hertfordshire boundary, south of Lyonsdown Road.**
         – On 6 December MET opens a line between Turnpike Lane and the eastern end of Alexandra Palace.
         – **On 22 December the line between Archway Tavern and Archway Bridge is opened.**

1906   – On 11 April MET extends the Bruce Grove Station–Wood Green line to the western end of Alexandra Palace.
         – **On 23 June there is a serious accident at Archway Road.**
         – **On 4 August the line Archway–Whetstone line is extended to the county boundary at Lyonsdown Road.**

    – On 10 October MET opens a line between Royal Oak, Harlesden and Iron Bridge at Stonebridge Park.

    – Stonebridge Depot is opened by MET in October at Brentfield Park.

    – **On 28 November MET opens a line between Green Lanes and The Ranelagh, Bounds Green Road.**

    – On 22 December MET opens a line between Harlesden Lock Bridge and Westbourne Park.

1907   – **On 28 March the line between Archway and the county boundary is extended to Barnet Church.**

    – **On 10 May the line between Green Lanes and The Ranelagh, Bounds Green is extended to Station Road, New Southgate at the junction with Friern Barnet Road and through running commences the next day.**

    – LCC opens Holloway tram depot.

    – **On 21 August Finchley depot is enlarged.**

    – On 28 November the LCC extends its electrified line from Highbury Station to Archway.

    – On 11 December MET opens a line between Tramway Avenue and Freezywater.

    – **On 23 December MET opens a line between Willesden Green and Dudden Hill.**

1908   – On 17 April Met extends the line between Tramway Avenue and Freezywater to Waltham Cross.

    – **On 3 June MET opens a line between Willesden Green and Willesden Junction.**

    – On 1 August MET opens a line between Palmers Green and Vicars Moor Lane, Winchmore Hill.

1909   – **On 8 April the line between Green Lanes and New Southgate is extended to North Finchley, Woodhouse Road.**

    – On 3 July MET extends the Palmers Green–Winchmore Hill line to Enfield GER Station.

    – On 25 September the first trolleybus to be built in Britain, a twenty-four seat single-decker, is demonstrated at METs Hendon Depot by Railless, although it never ran in public service.

    – **On 8 October the MET Willesden Green - Willesden Junction line is extended to Acton.**

    – **On 30 November the LCC line from Archway Tavern to Kentish Town is electrified.**

    – **On 16 December MET opens the line between North Finchley and Golders Green.**

1910   – **On 21 February MET extends the North Finchley–Golders Green line to Cricklewood.**

    – **On 21 February the Green Lanes–North Finchley, Woodhouse Road line is extended to Tally Ho corner.**

    – On 6 December the Harlesden Lock Bridge–Westbourne Park line is extended to Paddington.

    – On 6 December MET opens a line between Sudbury and Warwick Crescent.

1911   – On 20 February the Winchmore Hill–Enfield GER Station line is extended to Ponders End.

    – On 20 June Britain's first ever trolleybus runs in Leeds and Bradford.

1912   – 'The Combine' is formed, consisting of Underground Electric Railways Company, London General Omnibus Company, Tramways (MET) Omnibus Company, Gearless Omnibus Company, South Metropolitan Electric Tramways and Lighting Company.

    – MET tram services are numbered for the first time.

1913   – **In the Autumn Friern Barnet Road bridge is widened.**

    – On 23 November the North Finchley–Finsbury Park service is extended to Holborn.

1914   – **The change pit at Archway is opened on 24 September and service 38 is extended from Barnet Church - Archway Tavern to Moorgate and renumbered 9.**

    – The last horse bus runs in London.

1926   – The first six-wheeler double-deck trolleybus (a Guy) enters service in Wolverhampton.

1927   **– On 20 March experimental car No.318 (*Bluebell*) is introduced on service 40.**
      – On 17 June *Bluebell* crashes at Barnet Hill, killing the motorman.

1928   **– In spring *Bluebell* re-enters service after rebuilding.**

1929   **– In spring car No.320 enters service on route 40 (Whetstone–Cricklewood).**
      – On 6 November car No.330 enters service on Service 40 (Whetstone–Cricklewood).

1931   **– On 1 February the first Feltham tram enters service on Service 40 (Whetstone–Cricklewood).**
      – On 16 May London's first trolleybus service commences between Teddington and Twickenham.

1933   – On 1 July all tramcars, as well as buses and the Underground, pass into London Passenger Transport Board ownership.

1936   – On 31 July LPTB's parliamentary Bill receives Royal Assent, allowing conversion from tram to trolleybus.
      – On 2 August trolleybus routes 645 and 660 replace tram services 45 and 60.
      – *Bluebell* (now renumbered 2255 by LT) is withdrawn in August.
      – Stonebridge depot (SE) is extended for trolleybus operation.

1937   – On 5 March tram Service 21 is withdrawn and replaced on 6 March by trolleybus routes 521 and 621.

1938   **– On 5 March tram Service 45 is withdrawn and replaced on 6 March by trolleybus route 645.**
      – On 5 March tram Service 17 is withdrawn and replaced on 6 March by trolleybus route 517/617.
      – On 1 June trolleybus route 651 is replaced by route 645.

1950   – Hendon depot is renamed Colindale (CE) from July.
      – Holloway depot is renamed Highgate (HT).

1952   – On 5 July the last tram runs in London.

1961   **– On 31 January trolleybus routes 517/617 are withdrawn and replaced on 1 February by bus route 17.**
      – On 7 November trolleybus routes 521 to 621 are withdrawn and replaced on 8 November by bus route 221.
      – On 7 November trolleybus route 609 is withdrawn and replaced on 8 November by bus route 104.

1962   **– On 2 January the last trolleybuses run on routes 645 and 660 and are replaced by new bus routes 245 and 260.**
      – London's last trolleybus runs on 8 May.
      – Colindale depot (formerly Hendon) closes on 2 January.

1981   – Stonebridge depot is closed in August.

1993   **– Finchley depot closes on 3 December.**

APPENDIX 2

MET TRAM SERVICES

NO NUMBER. HIGHGATE (ARCHWAY BRIDGE) – WHETSTONE

- Via Archway Road, North Finchley
- Introduced Wednesday 7 June 1905
- Extended to Archway Tavern on Friday 22 December 1905
- Extended to New Barnet County Boundary on Saturday 4 August 1906
- Extended to Barnet Church on Thursday 28 March 1907
- Service numbered 38 from 1913

NO NUMBER. NORTH FINCHLEY – FINSBURY PARK

- Via Friern Barnet Road, New Southgate Station, Bounds Green Road, Wood Green, Turnpike Lane, Manor House
- Introduced Thursday 8 April 1909
- Service numbered 34 in 1913

NO NUMBER. NORTH FINCHLEY – GOLDERS GREEN

- Via Ballards Lane, Finchley Church End, Temple Fortune
- Introduced Thursday 16 December 1909
- Extended to Cricklewood Broadway via Cricklewood Lane on Monday 21 February 1910
- Service numbered 46 in 1912

SERVICE 9. BARNET CHURCH – MOORGATE

- Via Finchley Church End, East Finchley Station, Archway Road, Archway Tavern, Holloway Road, Nag's Head, Highbury Station, Upper Street, Cross Street, Islington Angel, Canal Bridge, City Road, Old Street
- Introduced Thursday 24 September 1914
- Journey time 50 minutes
- Service every 8 minutes
- Joint service operated by both MET and LCC cars
- Curtailed at North Finchley on Tuesday 1 December 1914
- Service operated by LT after July 1933
- Last day of operation Saturday 5 March 1938
- Replaced by trolleybus route 609

SERVICE 19. BARNET – TOTTENHAM COURT ROAD (EUSTON ROAD)

- Via Whetstone, North Finchley, East Finchley Station, Archway Road, Junction Road, Kentish Town, Camden Town, Hampstead Road
- Introduced Thursday 24 September 1914
- Journey time 58 minutes

- Service every 8 minutes
- Joint service operated by both MET and LCC cars
- Extended to Barnet Church on Tuesday 1 December 1914
- Service withdrawn on Monday 26 February 1917 and replaced by 38
- Service reintroduced on Monday 2 September 1918
- Service operated by LT after July 1933
- Last day of operation Saturday 5 March 1938
- Replaced by trolleybus route 517/617 between North Finchley and Holborn

SERVICE 21. NORTH FINCHLEY (WOODHOUSE ROAD) – HOLBORN

- Via New Southgate, Bounds Green Road, Wood Green, Turnpike Lane, Green Lanes, Manor House, Finsbury Park, Caledonian Road, King's Cross, Gray's Inn Road
- Introduced Thursday 8 April 1909
- Journey time 60 minutes
- Service every 3-5 minutes
- Joint service operated by both MET and LCC cars
- Service extended on Monday 24 September 1923 to Tally Ho Corner
- Service operated by LT after July 1933
- Last day of operation Saturday 5 March 1938
- Replaced by trolleybus routes 521/621

SERVICE 25. NEW SOUTHGATE – TOTTENHAM COURT ROAD

- Introduced Wednesday 29 March 1922
- Service withdrawn Wednesday 14 February 1923

SERVICE 34. NORTH FINCHLEY – WOOD GREEN

- Via New Southgate, Bounds Green Road
- Introduced Wednesday 2 May 1917
- Withdrawn Wednesday 27 October 1920

SERVICE 38. NORTH FINCHLEY – BARNET CHURCH

- Introduced 26 February 1917
- Withdrawn Monday 2 September 1918

SERVICE 40. NORTH FINCHLEY – CRICKLEWOOD

- Via Ballards Lane, Finchley Church End, Temple Fortune, Golders Green Station, Childs Hill, Cricklewood Tavern
- Introduced Monday 21 February 1910
- Service extended to Barnet weekday evenings in May 1926
- Service extended to Whetstone Sunday afternoons and evenings from October 1926
- Journey time 30 minutes
- Service every 8 minutes
- Service operated by LT after July 1933
- Service renumbered 45 on Wednesday 3 October 1934

SERVICE 42. WHETSTONE – CRICKLEWOOD (WEEKDAYS ONLY)

- Introduced 1913 as an extension of Service 40 and numbered 42

- Withdrawn in 1916 but reinstated in 1921
- From Monday 14 May 1923 service operated only in peak hours
- Service withdrawn in May 1926

SERVICE 44. BARNET – CRICKLEWOOD (SUNDAYS ONLY)

- Introduced 1912 as an extension of Service 40 and numbered 44
- On Thursday 11 October 1928 service is restricted to summer weekends only
- The North Finchley–Barnet section withdrawn in 1931

SERVICE 45. NORTH FINCHLEY - CRICKLEWOOD

- This was the former Service 40 which was renumbered 45 on Wednesday 3 October 1934
- Extended on Sunday 21 April 1935 on Sunday afternoons from Whetstone to Barnet Church
- Service withdrawn Saturday 1 August 1936
- Replaced by trolleybus route 645 on Sunday 2 August 1936

SERVICE 46. NORTH FINCHLEY – GOLDERS GREEN

- This number was allocated for short workings of Service 40
- Extended to Childs Hill Monday 14 May 1923
- Service withdrawn in May 1926

SERVICE 60. NORTH FINCHLEY – PADDINGTON

- Via Ballards Lane, Finchley Church End, Temple Fortune, Golders Green Station, Childs Hill, Cricklewood Tavern, Cricklewood The Crown, Willesden Green, Pound Lane, Church Road White Horse, Craven Park, Kensal Green, Royal Oak Station
- Introduced May 1923
- Journey time 63 minutes
- Service every 8 minutes.
- Service extended to Barnet summer Saturdays & Sundays in May 1926
- Journey time 87 minutes
- Service every 8 minutes
- Service operated by LT after July 1933
- Last day of operation Saturday 1 August 1936
- Replaced by trolleybus route 660 on Sunday 2 August 1936

SERVICE 69. NORTH FINCHLEY – TOTTENHAM COURT ROAD (EUSTON ROAD)

- Via East Finchley Station, Archway Road, Junction Road, Kentish Town, Camden Town, Hampstead Road
- Introduced 1920
- Journey time 45 minutes
- Operated weekday rush hours only
- Operated by LCC
- On Thursday 11 October 1928 withdrawn between North Finchley and East Finchley but reinstated on Sunday 11 August 1929
- Withdrawn Thursday 29 October 1931 and replaced by increased frequencies on services 9 and 19

WARNING: THE LONDON PASSENGER TRANSPORT BOARD WILL NOT BE RESPONSIBLE FOR ACCIDENTS CAUSED THROUGH PASSENGERS LEANING OVER THE SIDE OF THE CAR.

MET TRAM SPECIFICATIONS

Type (introduced)	MET Fleet numbers	Builder	Truck	Motors	Controller	Features
B & B2(1904 B, 1914–15 B2)	1–70	Brush	Brush	GE/BTH (2 x 40 hp)	BTH	B open top
A (1904–05)	71–130	Brush	Brush	GE (2 x 50 hp)	BTH	Open top (rebuilt 1928–29 with covered top)
C2 (1914–15)	151–165	Brush	Brush	GE (2 x 50 hp)	BTH	Covered top
D (1905–06)	166–191	Brush	Brush	GE (2 x 28 hp)	BTH	Open top
C/1 (1929)	192–211	MET/ LGOC	M&G	GE (2 x 60 hp)	BTH	Open top (rebuilt 1929 with covered top)
F (1908)	212–216	MET	Brush	GE (2 x 60 hp)	BTH	Covered top
G (1909)	217–236	MET	Brush	GE (2 x 50 hp)	BTH	Open top (rebuilt 1929–30 with covered top)
H (1909–12)	237–316	Brush	Brush	GE (2 x 60 hp)	BTH	Covered top
Bluebell (1926)	318	MET	MET	MV (2 x 50 hp)	BTH	Covered top
Feltham experimental (1929)	320	UCC	MET	MV (2 x 50 hp)	EE	Lightweight
Feltham experimental (1929)	330	UCC	Brush	BTH (2 x 50 hp)	EE	Pay-as-you enter
Feltham experimental (1930)	331	UCC	UCC	GE (4 x 35hp)	BTH	Centre-entrance only
Feltham (1931)	321–329 & 332–375	UCC	EMB	BTH (2 x 70 hp)	OK	Production models

Approx weight of cars 5 tons (open top), 8 tons (covered top). Feltham 18 tons 6 cwts.

BTH = British Thomson–Houston Co Ltd
EE = English Electric
GE = General Electric Company of England
M&G = Mountain & Gibson Ltd
MV = Metropolitan-Vickers Ltd
UCC = Union Construction Company Ltd

APPENDIX 4

Independent Motor Bus Routes

HORSE BUS. NO ROUTE NUMBER. FINCHLEY – CHARING CROSS

- Via East End, Dirt House, Highgate, Kentish Town, Camden Town, Park Street, York and Albany, Clarence Street, Albany Street, Portland Road, Great Portland Street, Oxford Street, Regent Circus, Piccadilly, Waterloo Place, Pall Mall, Cockspur Street
- As at May 1851
- Two buses per day each way
- Journey time 90 minutes

HORSE BUS. NO ROUTE NUMBER. HADLEY – GENERAL POST OFFICE

- Via Monken Hadley, Chipping Barnet, Whetstone, Finchley, Highgate Archway, Upper Holloway, Lower Holloway, Highbury Place, Upper Street, Broadway, Islington, High Street, Angel Inn, Goswell Street, Aldersgate Street, St Martins le Grand
- As at May 1851
- Six buses per day each way
- This was a mail omnibus

HORSE BUS. NO ROUTE NUMBER. TOTTERIDGE - HOLBORN

- Via Whetstone, Finchley, East End, Dirt House, Highgate, Highgate Archway, Upper Holloway, Lower Holloway, Highbury Place, Upper Street, Broadway, High Street, Angel, City Road
- As at May 1851
- One bus per day each way
- Journey time 2 hours

MOTOR BUS. NO ROUTE NUMBER. NORTH FINCHLEY – OXFORD CIRCUS

- Via Finchley Road, Swiss Cottage, Baker Street
- Operated by Birch Bros, then French Ltd, then T. Hearn
- Introduced 12 January 1905
- Withdrawn 23 October 1907

MOTOR BUS. NO ROUTE NUMBER. HADLEY HIGHSTONE – STRAND (LAW COURTS)

- Via Great North Road, Barnet High Street, Barnet Hill, Whetstone, North Finchley, Ballards Lane, Regents Park Road, Finchley Road, Wellington Road, Park Road, Baker Street, Oxford Street, Regent Street, Piccadilly Circus, Trafalgar Square
- Operated by Vanguard
- Introduced 10 March 1907
- Withdrawn October 1907

ROUTE 206. HADLEY HIGHSTONE – HAMPTON COURT

- Via High Barnet, Whetstone, North Finchley, East Finchley, Highgate, Archway, Tufnell Park, Kentish Town, Camden Town, Hampstead Road, Marylebone Road, Paddington, Westbourne Grove, Notting Hill Gate, Kensington High street, Hammersmith, Chiswick, Kew, Richmond, Twickenham, Teddington
- Operated by Adelaide (red & cream livery), Alberta (red & white livery), Birch Brothers (red & white livery), W.R. Drake (cream & black livery)
- Introduced 1 December 1924
- LGOC took over from Alberta on weekdays from 5 November 1926
- Last day of operation by LGOC 28 June 1927
- Birch Brothers acquired the W.R. Drake workings on 27 October 1928
- Route renumbered 227 in April 1929

ROUTE 206B. HADLEY HIGHSTONE – TWICKENHAM STATION

- This was the number allocated to a short working on route 206

ROUTE 206C. HADLEY HIGHSTONE – HAMMERSMITH

- This was the number allocated to a short working on route 206

ROUTE 206D. HADLEY HIGHSTONE – HIGHGATE

- This was the number allocated to a short working on route 206

ROUTE 227. HADLEY HIGHSTONE – HAMPTON COURT

- Via High Barnet, Whetstone, North Finchley, East Finchley, Highgate, Archway, Tufnell Park, Kentish Town, Camden Town, Hampstead Road, Marylebone Road, Paddington, Westbourne Grove, Notting Hill Gate, Kensington High Street, Hammersmith, Chiswick, Kew, Richmond, Twickenham, Teddington
- Operated by Adelaide (red & cream livery), Birch Brothers (red & white livery)
- Introduced April 1929
- Withdrawn 1 January 1931

ROUTE 227B. HADLEY HIGHSTONE – TWICKENHAM STATION

- This was the number allocated to a short working on route 227
- Withdrawn *c*.1931

ROUTE 227C. HADLEY HIGHSTONE – HAMMERSMITH

- This was the number allocated to a short working on route 227
- Withdrawn *c*.1931

ROUTE 227D. HADLEY HIGHSTONE – HIGHGATE

- This was the number allocated to a short working on route 227
- Withdrawn October 1930

ROUTE 227E. WHETSTONE – HAMPTON COURT

- This was the number allocated to a short working on route 227
- Introduced 20 April 1930
- Withdrawn 1 January 1933 (Adelaide taken over by LPTB)

ROUTE 274. NORTH FINCHLEY (SWAN & PYRAMIDS) – TOTTENHAM HALE

- Via Friern Barnet Road, New Southgate, Bounds Green Road, Wood Green, West Green Road, Broad Lane
- Operated by Admiral (navy blue livery)
- Introduced 1924
- Service believed withdrawn February 1925

ROUTE 279. HADLEY HIGHSTONE – LIVERPOOL STREET STATION

- Via Barnet, Whetstone, North Finchley, Ballards Lane, Golders Green, Childs Hill, Swiss Cottage, Baker Street, Oxford Circus, Piccadilly Circus, Trafalgar Square, Strand, Fleet Street, Cannon Street, Bank
- Operated by Burlington (chocolate & white livery), Carlton (red & white livery), Majestic, (chocolate & white livery), Overground (red & cream livery), Western (chocolate & white livery), X Service (khaki & red livery)
- X Service introduced between North Finchley and Golders Green on 20 Feb 1923 with no route number
- Numbered route introduced 1 December 1924
- All traces of route disappeared by 1929

ROUTE 279A. HADLEY HIGHSTONE – CHARING CROSS

- This was the number allocated to a short working on route 279

ROUTE 279B. NORTH FINCHLEY – STRAND

- Weekday morning peaks only
- This was the number allocated to a short working on route 279

ROUTE 279C. NORTH FINCHLEY – CHARING CROSS

- This was the number allocated to a short working on route 279

ROUTE 279D. GOLDERS GREEN – LIVERPOOL STREET

- This was the number allocated to a short working on route 279

ROUTE 279E. HADLEY HIGHSTONE - STRAND

- This was the number allocated to a short working on route 279
- Introduced 23 February 1927

ROUTE 279F. HADLEY HIGHSTONE – GOLDERS GREEN

- This was the number allocated to a short working on route 279
- Introduced 23 February 1927

ROUTE 284. HADLEY HIGHSTONE – VICTORIA (BUCKINGHAM PALACE ROAD)

- Via Barnet, Whetstone, North Finchley, East Finchley, Highgate, Archway, Tufnell Kentish Town, Camden, Town, Hampstead Road, Tottenham Court Road, Trafalgar Square, Westminster
- Introduced May 1924
- Operated by Cardinal (red & white livery), Carlton/Overground (red & cream livery), Claremont (red & white livery), Dauntless (red & white livery), Drake & McCowen (yellow & black livery), Hav-a-Ride/ HFB (red & white livery), Empires Best (red & white livery), The Leader, Sphere (red & white livery)
- Last operation by Hav-a-Ride 1927

ROUTE 284A. POTTERS BAR - VICTORIA

- This was the number allocated to a short working on route 284
- This was the main operation on the route
- Route renumbered 134 on 3 October 1934

ROUTE 284B. NORTH FINCHLEY (SWAN & PYRAMIDS) - VICTORIA

- This was the number allocated to a short working on route 284
- On 31 July 1930 this was redesignated as Hadley Highstone – Highgate

ROUTE 284C. HADLEY HIGHSTONE – CAMDEN TOWN

- This was the number allocated to a short working on route 284

ROUTE 284D. HADLEY HIGHSTONE – CHARING CROSS

- This was the number allocated to a short working on route 284

ROUTE 284E. HIGHGATE – CHARING CROSS

- This was the number allocated to a short working on route 284

ROUTE 285. BOREHAMWOOD (CROWN) – VICTORIA

- Via Barnet Gate, Arkley, Wood Street, High Barnet, Whetstone, North Finchley, East Finchley, Highgate, Archway, Tufnell Park, Kentish Town, Camden Town, Hampstead Road, Tottenham Court Road, Trafalgar Square, Westminster
- Operated by Overground (red & cream livery)
- Operated summer Sundays only
- Introduced 9 April 1930
- Withdrawn 3 October 1932 and renumbered 135

ROUTE 285A. ARKLEY (ARKLEY HOTEL) – VICTORIA (BUCKINGHAM PALACE ROAD)

- Via Wood Street, High Barnet, Whetstone, Friern Barnet Lane, Colney Hatch Lane, Muswell Hill Broadway, Muswell Hill Road, Highgate, Archway, Tufnell Park, Kentish Town, Camden Town, Hampstead Road, Tottenham Court Road, Trafalgar Square, Westminster
- Operated by Overground (red & cream livery)
- Introduced 9 April 1930
- Withdrawn 4 October 1932

ROUTE 285B. ARKLEY (ARKLEY HOTEL) – CHARING CROSS (TRAFALGAR SQUARE)

- This was the number allocated to a short working on route 285A
- Rerouted via Friern Barnet and Muswell Hill 5 October 1932
- Withdrawn 3 October 1934 and renumbered 135

ROUTE 285C. ARKLEY (ARKLEY HOTEL) – HIGHGATE (ARCHWAY STATION)

- This was the number allocated to a short working on route 285A
- Rerouted via Friern Barnet and Muswell Hill 5 October 1932
- Route renumbered 135 on 3 October 1934

ROUTE 307.ENFIELD TOWN – WHETSTONE (BLACK BULL)

- Via Windmill Hill, Oakwood, Cat Hill, East Barnet Village, Longmore Avenue, Great North Road
- Operated by Overground (red & cream livery)
- Introduced 13 March 1933
- Route renumbered 107 on 3 October 1934

ROUTE 519E. HADLEY HIGHSTONE (TWO BREWERS) – WOOD GREEN (LYMINGTON AVENUE)

- Via Barnet, Whetstone, Oakleigh Road, New Southgate, Bounds Green Road
- Operated by Barnet Motor Services (yellow & brown livery)
- Weekdays only (ten journeys each way)
- Introduced 2 June 1924
- Service curtailed at Bull & Butcher, Whetstone on 2 November 1924 (fifteen journeys each way), except Sundays where it operated to Hadley Highstone
- Renumbered 353 and extended to Totteridge War Memorial in January 1925
- Last day of operation by Barnet Motor Services December 1925
- Operated by Admiral (navy blue livery) until 1926
- Route later renumbered 354

ROUTE 521A. HADLEY HIGHSTONE – GOLDERS GREEN

- Via Barnet, Whetstone, North Finchley, Ballards Lane
- Operated by Western (chocolate and white livery)
- Introduced 6 April 1925
- Route renumbered 279F on 23 February 1927

ROUTE 521B. NORTH FINCHLEY (TALLY HO CORNER) – LONDON BRIDGE STATION

- Via Ballards Lane, Golders Green, Childs Hill, Swiss Cottage, Baker Street, Oxford Circus, Piccadilly Circus, Trafalgar Square, Strand, Fleet Street, Cannon Street, Bank, King William Street
- This was the number allocated to a short working on route 521
- Introduced 6 April 1925

ROUTE 521C. HADLEY HIGHSTONE - STRAND

- This was the number allocated to a short working on route 521
- Introduced 6 April 1925
- Route renumbered 279E on 23 February 1927

ROUTE 526. HADLEY HIGHSTONE – WANDSWORTH BRIDGE

- Via Barnet, Whetstone, North Finchley, Ballards Lane, Golders Green, Childs Hill, Cricklewood Broadway, Willesden Green, Craven Park, Harlesden, Victoria Road, Horn Lane Acton, Acton Vale, Shepherds Bush, Holland Road, Kensington Street, North End Road, Walham Green, Wandsworth Bridge Road
- Introduced 6 April 1925, but seldom, if ever, operated

ROUTE 526C. HADLEY HIGHSTONE – NORTH FINCHLEY (TALLY HO CORNER)

- Introduced 6 April 1925, but seldom, if ever, operated

ROUTE 526D. NORTH FINCHLEY – WANDSWORTH BRIDGE

- Via Golders Green, Cricklewood, Willesden, Harlesden, Acton, Shepherds Bush, Holland Road, North End Road, Walham Green
- Operated by Alma (red & white livery), Birch Bros (red & white livery), Clarence (red & white livery),
- Cornwall (red & white livery), Favourite (red & cream livery), FW, Glandfield, Lonsdale (red & white livery), Paragon (red livery), Pullman (red & white livery), Robert Thackray (red & white livery), The Royal (red & white livery), Royal Blue (royal blue & white livery), Tally Ho! (red & white livery), J D Thackray (red & white livery), Varsity (blue & white livery)
- Introduced 6 April 1925. This was the main route
- Favourite ceased operation in 1927
- Route renumbered 26 in 1934

ROUTE 551. WHETSTONE (THE GRIFFIN) - EDMONTON (SPARKLETS WORKS)

- Via Oakleigh Road, Bowes Road, new North Circular Road, Silver Street, Angel Road
- Operated by Astoria (crimson & cream livery), BB (dark red & white livery), H M Merry (red & white livery), HHC, Prince (chocolate & cream livery), Redburn (red & white livery), SB (red & white livery), Silver Star (red & white livery), Uneedus (red & white livery)
- Introduced July 1925 by Redburn
- Uneedus started operation in 1926
- Silver Star started operation 27 October 1926 and ceased 20 May 1927
- Operated by single-deck buses
- Extended to Totteridge (Barnet Lane) via Totteridge Lane on 16 October 1929
- Edmonton terminus changed from Sparklets Works to Cooks Ferry Inn on 17 December 1930
- Last day of operation on Sunday 20 March 1932

ROUTE 551B. TOTTERIDGE (BARNET LANE) – EDMONTON (PARK ROAD)

- This was the number allocated to an extended working on route 551

ROUTE 551D. BURNT OAK (EDGWARE ROAD) – EDMONTON (PARK ROAD)

- Route 551 Extended Monday to Saturday from Totteridge to Burnt Oak (Edgware Road) via Totteridge Lane, Highwood Hill, Lawrence Street, Mill Hill Broadway, Watling Avenue on 9 August 1933. Withdrawn between Arnos Grove Station and Edmonton (Cooks Ferry Inn) on 16 May 1934
- Route renumbered 251 on 3 October 1934

The Bassom system of numbering routes with letter suffixes was introduced in 1924 by Chief Constable Bassom. The main route number was allocated to the longest part of a route and short workings were each given a different letter suffix. This was a logical but cumbersome system and was subsequently dismantled on 3 October 1934 by the LPTB who allocated just one number for each route and its variations.

APPENDIX 5
LGOC ('GENERAL') BUS ROUTES

ROUTE 2. NORTH FINCHLEY (SWAN & PYRAMIDS) – CATFORD

- Via Golders Green Station, Finchley Road, Park Lane, Victoria, Vauxhall, Brixton, Herne Hill, West Norwood, Crystal Palace, Sydenham
- Introduced 16 February 1913
- Extended weekday peak hours to Arnos Grove Station via High Road, Oakleigh Road North, Oakleigh Road South
- On Mondays – Saturdays route ran in two sections North Finchley – Norwood and Golders Green – Catford
- Withdrawn between Golders Green Station and Arnos Grove Station 12 February 1946

ROUTE 29B. NORTH FINCHLEY (SWAN & PYRAMIDS) – VICTORIA

- Via Woodhouse Road, Friern Barnet Road, Bounds Green Road, Wood Green, Green Lanes, Seven Sisters Road, Camden Road, Charing Cross Road
- Introduced 12 September 1923
- Withdrawn 29 November 1924
- Route renumbered 129 from 1 December 1924
- Last day of operation 8 April 1930

ROUTE 34. WHETSTONE (GRIFFIN) – STRATFORD BROADWAY

- Via Oakleigh Road North, Oakleigh Road South, Arnos Grove, Palmers Green, Edmonton, North Circular Road, Walthamstow, Leyton High Road, Crownfield Road, Maryland Point
- Introduced 3 October 1934

ROUTE 43. FRIERN BARNET (ORANGE TREE) – LONDON BRIDGE STATION

- Via Hampden Road, Muswell Hill Broadway, Highgate Archway, Kingsdown Road, Angel Islington
- Introduced 7 December 1921

ROUTE 43A. COLNEY HATCH LANE (WILTON ROAD) – LONDON BRIDGE STATION

- Via Muswell Hill, Fortis Green, East Finchley, Highgate, Holloway, Highbury, Islington, Moorgate
- Introduced 7 December 1914 (up to then it had only run as far as Muswell Hill)
- Last day of operation 21 March 1937

ROUTE 43B. ARKLEY (ARKLEY HOTEL) – SOUTH CROYDON (SWAN & SUGAR LOAF)

- Via Wood Street, High Barnet, Barnet Hill, Great North Road, Whetstone, North Finchley, East Finchley, Highgate Archway, Holloway, Islington, City Road, Moorgate, Bank, London Bridge, Elephant & Castle, Kennington, Brixton, Streatham, Norbury, Croydon

- Sundays only
- Introduced 1 December 1924
- Last day of operation 30 September 1934

ROUTE 43C. COLNEY HATCH LANE (WILTON ROAD) – STREATHAM COMMON

- Short working of route 43
- Introduced 1 December 1924
- Extended on 24 November 1926 to South Croydon (Swan & Sugar Loaf) – Friern Barnet (Orange Tree)
- Extended 2 January 1929 to Whetstone (Black Bull) on Sundays
- Last day of operation 6 April 1930

ROUTE 71. FINSBURY PARK STATION – ST ALBANS (MARKET PLACE)

- Via Manor House, Harringay, Wood Green, Bounds Green, New Southgate, Friern Barnet Road, Woodhouse Road, North Finchley, Whetstone, Great North Road, Barnet Hill, High Barnet, South Mimms, London Colney
- Introduced 1 July 1923
- Last day of operation 1 October 1933

ROUTE 71A. FINSBURY PARK STATION – NORTH FINCHLEY (TALLY HO)

- Short working on route 71
- Introduced 3 June 1925
- Last day of operation 1 August 1932

ROUTE 82. GOLDERS GREEN STATION – HATFIELD (DRAY HORSE)

- Via Finchley Central, North Finchley, Whetstone, Great North Road, Barnet, Potters Bar, Bell Bar
- Introduced 6 May 1923
- Last day of operation 16 October 1927

ROUTE 84. GOLDERS GREEN STATION – ST ALBANS (RISING SUN)

- Via Temple Fortune, Finchley Central, Ballards Lane, North Finchley, Whetstone, Great North Road, Barnet Hill, High Barnet, South Mimms, London Colney
- Introduced 3 August 1912

ROUTE 87. COLNEY HATCH LANE (WILTON ROAD) – CLAPTON POND

- Via Muswell Hill, Fortis Green, East Finchley, Great North Road, Highgate, Holloway, Finsbury Park, Lordship Park, Stoke Newington, Northwold Road, Lower Clapton Road
- Introduced 19 August 1912
- Last day of operation 28 March 1914

ROUTE 106. FRIERN BARNET (ORANGE TREE) – LEYTONSTONE STATION

- Via Colney Hatch Lane, Muswell Hill, Fortis Green, East Finchley, Great North Road, Highgate Archway, Holloway, Seven Sisters Road, Finsbury Park, Blackstock Road, Lordship Park, Stoke Newington, Northwold Road, Clapton, Lea Bridge Road, Church Road Leyton, Leyton High Road, Union Road, High Road Leytonstone
- Introduced 29 March 1914 as replacement for route 87
- Route was cut back to Finsbury Park – Leytonstone Station on 31 October 1914

ROUTE 129. NORTH FINCHLEY (SWAN & PYRAMIDS) – VICTORIA STATION

- Via Woodhouse Road, Friern Barnet Road, New Southgate, Bounds Green, Harringay, Manor House, Seven Sisters Road, Holloway, Camden Road, Camden Town, Tottenham Court Road, Trafalgar Square, Westminster
- Introduced 1 December 1924
- Last day of operation 8 April 1930

ROUTE 155. GOLDERS GREEN STATION – HATFIELD (DRAY HORSE)

- Via Temple Fortune, Finchley Central, North Finchley, Whetstone, Great North Road, Barnet Hill, Barnet, Hadley Highstone, Potters Bar, Bell Bar, Great North Road
- Sundays only
- Introduced 17 May 1914
- Last day of operation 2 November 1919

After 1 July 1933 General routes were taken over by London Passenger Transport Board (LPTB) and thereafter buses carried the fleet name 'London Transport'.

APPENDIX 6

TROLLEYBUS ROUTES

ROUTE 517. NORTH FINCHLEY – HOLBORN CIRCUS

- Via East Finchley, Archway Road, Highgate Archway, Holloway, Caledonian Road, King's Cross, Gray's Inn Road (on northbound journeys via Farringdon Road)

ROUTE 617. NORTH FINCHLEY – HOLBORN CIRCUS

- Via East Finchley, Archway Road, Highgate Archway, Holloway, Caledonian Road, King's Cross, Farringdon Road (on northbound journeys via Gray's Inn Road)
- Introduced Monday 7 March 1938. Replaced tram route 17 (Archway – Farringdon Street)
- Journey time 43 minutes
- Service 3-6 minutes
- Operated by Finchley depot
- Last day of operation Tuesday 31 Jan 1961
- Replaced by bus route 17

ROUTE 521. NORTH FINCHLEY – HOLBORN CIRCUS

- Via New Southgate, Bounds Green Station, Wood Green Station, Turnpike Lane Station, Green Lanes, Manor House Station, Finsbury Park Station, Holloway Road, Nag's Head, Caledonian Road, King's Cross, Gray's Inn Road (on northbound journeys via Farringdon Road)

ROUTE 621. NORTH FINCHLEY – HOLBORN CIRCUS

- Via New Southgate, Bounds Green Station, Wood Green Station, Turnpike Lane Station, Green Lanes, Manor House Station, Finsbury Park Station, Holloway Road, Nag's Head, Caledonian Road, King's Cross, Farringdon Road (on northbound journeys via Gray's Inn Road)
- Introduced Sunday 6 March 1938. Replaced tram route 21
- Journey time 55 minutes
- Service every 3-6 minutes
- Operated by Finchley depot
- Last day of operation Tuesday 7 November 1961
- Replaced by bus route 221

ROUTE 609. BARNET CHURCH - MOORGATE

- Via Whetstone, North Finchley, East Finchley Station, Highgate, Archway, Holloway Nag's Head, Highbury, Islington Angel, City Road
- Introduced Sunday 6 March 1938. Replaced tram route 9
- Journey time 59 minutes
- Service every 4-8 minutes
- Operated by Finchley and Holloway/Highgate depots

- Last day of operation Tuesday 7 November 1961
- Replaced by bus route 104

ROUTE 645. BARNET CHURCH – CANONS PARK

- Via North Finchley, Finchley Church End, Temple Fortune, Golders Green, Childs Hill, Cricklewood Broadway, West Hendon, Colindale, Edgware Station Road
- Introduced Sunday 2 August 1936. Replaced tram routes 40 & 60
- Journey time 64 minutes
- Service every 6-10 minutes.
- Operated by Colindale and Finchley depots
- Last day of operation Tuesday 2 January 1962
- Replaced by bus routes 245/260

ROUTE 651. BARNET CHURCH – GOLDERS GREEN

- Via Whetstone, North Finchley, Finchley Church End, Temple Fortune. Extended Mon – Fri (except peaks) to Cricklewood via Childs Hill
- Introduced Sunday 6 Mach 1938. Replaced tram route 40
- Operated by Finchley depot
- Last day of operation Tuesday 31 May 1938
- Replaced by trolleybus route 645

ROUTE 660. NORTH FINCHLEY - HAMMERSMITH

- Via Finchley Church End, Temple Fortune, Golders Green, Childs Hill, Cricklewood St Gabriel's Church, Willesden Green, Craven Park, Harlesden, North Acton, Acton Vale, Askew Road
- Introduced Sunday 2 August 1936. Replaced tram route 60
- Journey time 69 minutes
- Service every 6-10 minutes
- Operated by Finchley and Stonebridge Park depots
- Last day of operation Tuesday 2 January 1962
- Replaced by bus route 260

APPENDIX 7
TROLLEYBUS SHORT WORKINGS

In order to try and keep to schedules, trolleybuses were often turned short of their original destinations. The following dedicated turning points were used:

517/617

North Finchley
East Finchley Station (northbound and southbound)
Archway, Macdonald Road (northbound only)
Holloway, Nag's Head (southbound only)
King's Cross (southbound only)

521/621

New Southgate (northbound only)
Wood Green (northbound and southbound)
Turnpike Lane (northbound only)
Finsbury Park (southbound only)
Holloway, Nag's Head (southbound only)
King's Cross (southbound only)

609

North Finchley (northbound and southbound)
East Finchley (northbound and southbound)
Archway, Macdonald Road (northbound only)
Holloway, Nag's Head (southbound only)
Islington Green (northbound and southbound)
Windsor Terrace, City Road (southbound only)

645

North Finchley (northbound and southbound)
Holly Park (northbound only: battery turn)
Golders Green Station (southbound only)
Cricklewood, St Gabriel's Church (northbound and southbound)
Colindale Depot (northbound and southbound)
Edgware, Station Road (northbound and southbound)

660

Holly Park (northbound only: battery turn)
Golders Green Station (southbound only)
Cricklewood Lane, Gillingham Road (northbound only)
Cricklewood, St Gabriel's Church (southbound only)
Craven Park (northbound and southbound)
North Acton (northbound and southbound)
Acton Market Place (northbound and southbound)
Bromyard Avenue, Acton Vale (southbound only)
Paddenswick Road (southbound only)

Grateful thanks to Hugh Taylor for supplying this information.

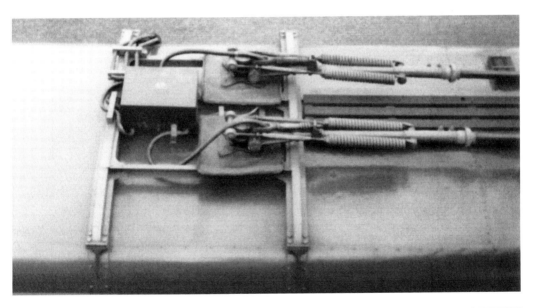

TROLLEYBUS SPECIFICATIONS & ALLOCATIONS

Class (introduced)	Fleet Nos	Chassis	Motor	Body	Local Depot Allocation (route)
C1 (1935–36)	132–183	AEC	English Electric (80 hp)	Weymann	Stonebridge Park (660) Holloway/Highgate (609)
C2,C3 (1936)	184–383	AEC	English Electric (80 hp)	BRCW/MCW	Colindale (645) Finchley (517/617,521/621, 645)
E1 (1937)	554–603	AEC	English Electric (95 hp)	Brush/Park Royal/Weymann	Stonebridge Park (660)
F1 (1937)	654–753	Leyland	Metrovick (95 hp)	Leyland	Stonebridge Park (660)
X4 (1937)	754	AEC	Metrovick (95 hp)	LPTB	Finchley (521/621,609)
H (1937–38)	755–904	Leyland	Metrovick (95 hp)	MCW	Holloway/Highgate (517/617,609)
J1 (1938)	905–951	AEC	Metrovick (95 hp)	BRCW/MCW/Weymann	Finchley (517/617/521/621,651)
J2,J3 (1938)	955–1054	AEC	English Electric (95 hp)	BRCW/MCW/Weymann	Finchley (521/621, 651, 609) Holloway/Highgate (517/617,609)
K1, K2 (1938)	1055–1354	Leyland	Metrovick (95 hp)	Leyland	Holloway/Highgate (517/617,609)
L1, L2, L3 (1939–40)	1355–1529	AEC	Metrovick (95 hp)	MCW	Finchley (521/631,660)
					Holloway/Highgate (517/617,609)
M1 (1939)	1530–1554	AEC	Metrovick (95 hp)	MCW	Finchley (521/621,645)
					Holloway/Highgate (517/617,609)
N1,N2 (1939)	1555–1669	AEC	Metrovick (95 hp)	BRCW/ Park Royal	Colindale (645) Finchley (521/621)
					Holloway/Highgate (609) Stonebridge Park (660)

BRCW = Birmingham Railway Carriage & Wagon Co. Ltd
MCW = Metropolitan–Cammell–Weymann Motor Bodies Ltd

RECOMMENDED READING

There are many excellent books on the subject that go into far more detail than has been possible here. Anyone interested in more comprehensive descriptions of the vehicles themselves and the systems is advised to consult the following:

Ken Blacker: *The London Trolleybus Vol. 1 1931-1945*. Capital Transport 2002.

Ken Blacker: *The London Trolleybus Vol. 2 1946-1962*. Capital Transport 2004.

Ken Blacker, Ron Lunn, Reg Westgate: *London's Buses Volume One*. H.J. Publications 1977.

Terence Cooper: *The Wheels Used to Talk to Us*. Tallis Publishing 1977.

John R. Day: *London's Trams and Trolleybuses*. London Transport 1977.

Ken Glazier: *The Battles of the General*. Capital Transport 2003.

Robert J. Harley: *LCC Electric Tramways*. Capital Transport 2002.

Robert J. Harley: *North London Trams*. Capital Transport 2008.

E.R. Oakley: *London County Council Tramways Vol. 2 North London*. London Tramways History Group 1991.

E.R. Oakley & C.E. Holland: *London Transport Tramways 1933-1952*. London Tramways History Group 1998.

Nicholas Owen: *History of the British Trolleybus*. David & Charles 1974.

C.S. Smeeton: *The Metropolitan Electric Tramways Vol. 1 – Origins to 1920*. Light Rail Transit Association 1984.

C.S. Smeeton: *The Metropolitan Electric Tramways Vol. 2 – 1921 to 1933*. Light Rail Transit Association 1984.

Hugh Taylor: *London Trolleybus Routes*. Capital Transport 1994.

Hugh Taylor: *London Trolleybuses: A Class Album*. Capital Transport 2006.

Mick Webber: *London Trolleybus Chronology 1931-1962*. Ian Allan 1997.

The seminal work on the history of London Transport is in two volumes, both sadly long out of print:

T.C. Barker and Michael Robbins: *A History of London Transport Vol. 1: The Nineteenth Century*. George Allen & Unwin 1963.

T.C. Barker and Michael Robbins: *A History of London Transport Vol. 2: The Twentieth Century to 1970*. George Allen & Unwin 1974.

TRANSPORT MUSEUMS

EAST ANGLIA TRANSPORT MUSEUM*

Chapel Road
Carlton Colville
Lowestoft
Suffolk
NR33 8BL
Telephone: 01502 518459
www.eatm.org.uk

Vehicles include London trolleybuses 260, 1201, 1521 and motor buses RT 3125 and RTL 1050.

LONDON TRANSPORT MUSEUM

Covent Garden Plaza
London
WC2E 7BB
Telephone: 020 7279 6344
www.ltmuseum.co.uk

Vehicles on display include Trolleybus 1253 and West Ham Corporation tram No. 102.

LT MUSEUM DEPOT

2 Museum Way
118-120 Gunnersbury Lane
London
W3 9BQ

This houses London Transport Museum's reserve collection of 370,000 items including tube trains, buses and the London Transport poster collection. The Depot is open to the public on a limited number of days each year although tours for groups can be arranged. For details contact London Transport Museum.

NATIONAL TRAMWAY MUSEUM*

Crich Tramway Village
Nr Matlock
Derbyshire
DE4 5DP
Telephone: 01773 854321
www.tramway.co.uk

Vehicles include LPTB No.1, LCC No.106, LUT No.159 and MET 331.

THE TROLLEYBUS MUSEUM*

Belton Road
Sandtoft
Doncaster
DN8 5SX
Telephone: 01724 711391
www.sandtoft.org

Among many trolleybuses here is London trolleybus No.1812.

Please note: Vehicles at the museums marked with a * are in working condition although not all the vehicles may be in operation. Check with the museums for details.

Other titles published by The History Press

Top-Deck Travel:
A History of Britain's Open-Top Buses
PHILIP C. MILES

This illustrated history charts the development of the open-top bus, from the early 1900s when buses ordinarily had an open top-deck to the bustling sightseeing operations so popular around the world today, recalling many operators along the way who have since been relegated to the annals of history.

ISBN 978 0 7524 5137 4

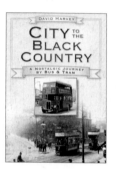

City to the Black Country:
A Nostalgic Journey by Bus & Tram
DAVID HARVEY

This fascinating collection of archive photographs takes the reader on a nostalgic bus and tram ride through the north-west of Birmingham, from the city centre along the A41 to Hockley, and is full of enough detail to delight local residents and transport enthusiasts alike.

ISBN 978 07524 5297 5

Directory of British Tramways Volume Three:
Northern England, Scotland and the Isle of Man
KEITH TURNER

This illustrated book is a practical and useful tool in revealing the tramway lines and networks of the British Isles, with archive photographs and informative text. Author Keith Turner's in-depth research and stunning illustrations offers the definitive work on the subject, following Volumes One and Two.

ISBN 978 18607 4239 6

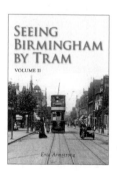

Seeing Birmingham by Tram Volume II
ERIC ARMSTRONG

Following closely the 1937 routes depicted in Volume I and including the fares structure, this book is illustrated with a wealth of fascinating archive postcards and ephemera depicting tramways operation of the era and placing an emphasis on the tram in its social and historical context. A must for all Birmingham transport and local historians!

ISBN 978 18607 5392 7

Visit our website and discover thousands of other History Press books.

www.thehistorypress.co.uk